OCS STUDY MMS 2005-035

Final Report

Distribution and Movements of Beluga Whales from the Eastern Chukchi Sea Stock During Summer and Early Autumn

by

Robert S. Suydam[1]

Lloyd F. Lowry[2]

Kathryn J. Frost[2]

[1]North Slope Borough Department of Wildlife Management
Box 69
Barrow, AK 99723
email: robert.suydam@north-slope.org

[2]Institute of Marine Science
School of Fisheries and Ocean Sciences
University of Alaska Fairbanks
Fairbanks, AK 99775-7220
(present mailing address: 1550 Coyote Trail, Fairbanks, AK 99701)

July 2005

PROJECT ORGANIZATION

This report includes data from two efforts to satellite tag beluga whales. The first was conducted by the Alaska Beluga Whale Committee (ABWC) through NOAA grant NA67FX0197, the Alaska Department of Fish and Game (ADF&G), the National Marine Fisheries Service (NMFS), the North Slope Borough (NSB), and the Village of Point Lay. This was the first time belugas in Alaska were instrumented with satellite tags. Ten belugas were tagged in 1998–1999. The second took place in 2000–2002. It was initiated by the ABWC and further supported by Minerals Management Service (MMS) through the Coastal Marine Institute. Other cooperators included NMFS, ADF&G, the NSB, the Village of Point Lay, and Alaska Marine Ecosystems Research.

Minerals Management Service through the Coastal Marine Institute provided funding to purchase 9 satellite tags, data acquisition from Service Argos and some travel funds. The NSB provided funds for the salary for one of the principal investigators, Robert Suydam, as well as funding for field travel and logistics support. ADF&G provided salaries for principal investigators Kathy Frost and Lloyd Lowry while they were employed by ADF&G and for Lori Quakenbush to participate in field work, as well as additional support for travel, supplies and data acquisition. The ABWC contributed funds for travel, the purchase of satellite transmitters, logistics support, and tagging supplies. Alaska Marine Ecosystems Research contributed the salaries for Kathy Frost and Lloyd Lowry for all work conducted after December 2000. The NMFS National Marine Mammal Laboratory assisted in fieldwork and with permitting.

The NSB and ADF&G had joint responsibility for project management. The NSB Department of Wildlife Management arranged logistics, coordinated fieldwork and acted as a liaison with the Village of Point Lay. ADF&G assisted in project planning, fieldwork and data analysis. Principal investigator Robert Suydam is a PhD candidate at the University of Washington and will include data from this study as part of his doctoral thesis. The University of Alaska Fairbanks coordinated accounting and reporting aspects of this study. All cooperators had input into project design, and have access to, and will be able to make use of, all data collected.

Robert Suydam (NSB Department of Wildlife Management, PhD student at University of Washington) was one of the Principal Investigators for this project. He supervised and coordinated all field aspects of this project, acted as the primary liaison with the Village of Point Lay and Point Lay hunters, and participated in data analysis and was primarily responsible for report preparation and presentation of results at conferences and meetings.

Kathryn J. Frost (ADF&G, now retired and affiliated with University of Alaska Fairbanks) was one of the Principal Investigators for this project. She participated in all aspects of the study including fieldwork, data acquisition and analysis and report preparation.

Lloyd F. Lowry (ADF&G, now retired and affiliated with University of Alaska Fairbanks) was one of the Principal Investigators for this project. He participated in the study design, mapping, analysis and interpretation of data and report writing.

TABLE OF CONTENTS

PROJECT ORGANIZATION i

LIST OF TABLES ii

LIST OF FIGURES ii

ABSTRACT 1

INTRODUCTION 2

OBJECTIVES AND HYPOTHESES 3

METHODS 4

    Capturing and Tagging of Whales 4

    Satellite Tag Data Analysis 5

RESULTS 6

    Capture and Tagging 6

    Movement Patterns 6

    Distribution Relative to Bathymetry and Ice Cover 8

    Distribution Relative to the Beaufort Sea Outer Continental Shelf Lease Areas 8

DISCUSSION 8

    Tag attachments and longevity 8

    Movements and distribution 9

    Gender- and age-related differences in movements 11

    Movements in relation to ice and bathymetry 12

    Use of the Beaufort Sea Outer Continental Shelf Lease Sale Area 13

ACKNOWLEDGMENTS 14

STUDY PRODUCTS 15

REFERENCES 16

LIST OF TABLES

Table 1. Beluga whales instrumented with tags at Point Lay, Alaska in 1998, 1999, 2001 and 2002 34

Table 2. Number of average daily locations of satellite tagged belugas within the Beaufort Sea OCS lease sale area, by longitude 35

LIST OF FIGURES

Figure 1. Configurations of satellite data recorders deployed on beluga whales in the eastern Chukchi Sea in 1998, 1999, 2001 and 2002 36

Figure 2.   Locations of beluga whales satellite tagged at Point Lay, Alaska, 8 July–10 October 1998 37

Figure 3.   Locations of beluga whales satellite tagged at Point Lay, Alaska, 30 June–24 September 1999 38

Figure 4.   Locations of beluga whales satellite tagged at Point Lay, Alaska, 3 July–5 December 2001 39

Figure 5.   Locations of beluga whales satellite tagged at Point Lay, Alaska, 7 July–29 September 2002 40

Figure 6.   Locations of beluga whales satellite tagged at Point Lay, Alaska in June and July 41

Figure 7.   Locations of beluga whales satellite tagged at Point Lay, Alaska in August 42

Figure 8.   Locations of beluga whales satellite tagged at Point Lay, Alaska in September 43

Figure 9.   Locations of beluga whales satellite tagged at Point Lay, Alaska in October–December 44

Figure 10. Locations of female belugas satellite tagged at Point Lay, Alaska, by age class 45

Figure 11. Locations of male belugas satellite tagged at Point Lay, Alaska, by age class 46

Figure 12. Locations of all belugas satellite tagged at Point Lay, Alaska, 1998–2002, in relation to Beaufort Sea OSC lease sale areas 47

Figure 13. Scars on the dorsum of a beluga at a transmitter attachment site 48

ABSTRACT

At least five stocks of beluga whales (*Delphinapterus leucas*) occur in Alaska. One of these stocks, the eastern Chukchi Sea stock, is most commonly seen in coastal waters near Kasegaluk Lagoon in northwestern Alaska during June and July. Despite protection under the Marine Mammal Protection Act and their importance to many Alaska Native hunters for subsistence, relatively little is known about the movements and seasonal distribution of these whales during the rest of the year. During 1998–2002 we instrumented 23 belugas with satellite-linked depth recorders (SDRs), including 12 adult males, 5 immature males, 2 adult females and 4 immature females. SDRs provided location information for an average of 67 (range 5–154) days. Saddle mount tags averaged 52 days, spider mounts 68 days and side mounts 81 days, although there was no statistical difference in longevity among attachment types. Animals moved north and east into the northern Chukchi and western Beaufort Sea after capture. During July–September, movement patterns differed by age and/or sex. All belugas that moved north of 75°N in the Beaufort Sea and Arctic Ocean were males. Adult males tended to use deeper water and to remain there for most of the summer. Five of nine adult males tagged from all-male groups early in their northward migration traveled through 90% pack ice cover to reach 79°N–80°N by late July/early August. Adult males captured from groups that included adult females also moved into deep water but apparently for shorter periods of time. In all years, adult and immature females remained at or near the shelf break throughout summer and early fall. Immature males moved farther north than immature females, but not as far north as adult males based on our small sample size. Belugas of all ages and both sexes were most often found in water deeper than 200m along and beyond the continental shelf break. They rarely used the inshore waters within the Outer Continental Shelf lease sale area of the Beaufort Sea. Heavy ice apparently did not inhibit the movements of large adult males in summer since they traveled through and were often located in >90% ice cover. Only three tagged belugas transmitted data after October. Those animals migrated south through the Bering Strait into the northern Bering Sea north of Saint Lawrence Island.

Key words: beluga whale, *Delphinapterus leucas*, Arctic Ocean, Beaufort Sea, Chukchi Sea, movements, oil and gas development, satellite telemetry

INTRODUCTION

Beluga whales (*Delphinapterus leucas*) occur throughout northern and western Alaska and are an important subsistence resource for Alaska Natives; approximately 300 belugas are harvested annually. Whales from northern and western Alaska may migrate through Alaskan, Russian and Canadian waters and are a subject of increasing interest in international cooperative management. Many belugas may migrate through or occur in offshore oil and gas leasing areas in Alaska and Canada. Concerns about potential effects of offshore oil and gas exploration and development on beluga whales exist at local, national, and international levels. Studies funded by the Outer Continental Shelf Environmental Assessment Program (OCSEAP) and the Minerals Management Service (MMS) in the early 1980s provided information about beluga reproduction (Burns and Seaman 1986), food habits (Seaman et al., 1982), and distribution and abundance in summer (Frost and Lowry, 1990). More recently studies conducted by the Alaska Beluga Whale Committee (ABWC), the Alaska Department of Fish and Game (ADF&G), the National Marine Fisheries Service (NMFS) and the North Slope Borough (NSB) have provided information about harvest levels, stock identity and genetic characteristics (O'Corry-Crowe et al., 1997, 2002), abundance in summering areas (Lowry and Frost 1998, Lowry et al., 1999 a,b), and satellite tracking (Suydam et al., 2001). Despite the importance of belugas as a subsistence resource and their protection under the Marine Mammal Protection Act, late summer distribution and fall migration patterns are poorly known, wintering areas are effectively unknown, and areas that are particularly important for feeding have not been identified.

In Alaska, there are at least five stocks of beluga whales. These stocks were initially identified based on traditional summering areas (Frost and Lowry, 1990) and later confirmed with genetic analysis (O'Corry-Crowe et al., 1997, 2002). Two of these stocks, the eastern Beaufort Sea and the eastern Chukchi Sea stocks, occur seasonally in the Beaufort Sea. The Beaufort Sea stock migrates north and east along the spring lead in April and May from the Bering Sea to the eastern Beaufort Sea and returns west through the Beaufort Sea in September and October (Richard et al., 2001b). Beluga whales of the eastern Chukchi Sea stock are most common in Kotzebue Sound and near Kasegaluk Lagoon in early summer (Frost and Lowry, 1990). Whales apparently have been using the Kasegaluk Lagoon region during summer for many years. Warren Neakok described hunting them there in about 1930 (Neakok et al., 1985). In recent years, the occurrence of belugas at Kasegaluk Lagoon has been quite predictable, and they usually arrive in late June or early July (Frost and Lowry, 1990; Huntington et al., 1999). The latest sightings of belugas near the lagoon usually occur in mid- to late July (Frost and Lowry, 1990; Huntington et al., 1999) and the distribution and movements of the whales after that time were completely unknown prior to satellite tracking (this study; Suydam et al., 2001). Before satellite tracking, we suspected that they moved north and spent the summer along the edge of the pack ice in the Chukchi or western Beaufort seas.

Understanding movements, distribution and behavior of wildlife, especially marine mammals, has been greatly enhanced through the use of technology. Frost et al. (1985) first used telemetry to study the movements and behavior of belugas. They attached VHF radios to the dorsal ridges of two belugas in Bristol Bay, Alaska, and tracked their movements for about two weeks. Subsequently, similar techniques have been used to attach satellite-linked transmitters to belugas in many areas of the Arctic (Martin et al., 1993; Smith and Martin, 1994; Richard et al.,

1997, 1998a,b, 2001a,b; Lydersen et al., 2001, Suydam et al., 2001). Satellite-linked transmitters have allowed researchers to track belugas over large areas and long periods of time. More belugas have been instrumented with satellite transmitters than any other species of cetacean (Reeves and St. Aubin, 2001). Satellite tagging offers a proven, cost-effective and technologically sound approach to obtaining information on beluga distribution and movements.

An annual subsistence drive hunt for belugas at Point Lay, Alaska, offers a good opportunity to capture and tag belugas from the eastern Chukchi Sea stock. Residents of Point Lay, adjacent to Kasegaluk Lagoon, drive belugas into the lagoon to a traditional hunting location. This situation provides opportunities to capture belugas that remain alive in the lagoon after the hunt. The ABWC initiated a satellite tracking study at Point Lay and successfully tracked a total of nine adult males and one immature female in 1998 (Suydam et al., 2001) and 1999. The Minerals Management Service (MMS), through the Coastal Marine Institute provided additional support for tagging more belugas, especially females and immature males, in subsequent years.

This study increases our knowledge of the movements and behavior of beluga whales from the eastern Chukchi Sea stock. Understanding the distribution and timing of movements of these belugas will be important for planning future lease sales in the Beaufort Sea and designing possible mitigation measures. It will support pre-lease information needs on marine mammal species that are potentially affected by industrial activities and will develop information that addresses public concerns about the general lack of knowledge about beluga whale distribution and ecology. It is especially important to gather this information because of the prominence of beluga whales in Alaskan Native culture and subsistence practices. In this paper, we present results from the project initiated by the ABWC, and further supported by MMS, to live-capture and attach satellite-linked depth recorders (SDRs) to belugas. We worked cooperatively with people from the village of Point Lay from 1996 to 2002 to capture and tag belugas in Kasegaluk Lagoon.

OBJECTIVES AND HYPOTHESES

Our primary objective was to track movements of belugas of the eastern Chukchi Sea stock once they leave the area of Kasegaluk Lagoon. In this report, we have summarized and compared data from 1998, 1999, 2001 and 2002.

Our specific hypotheses were:
- Belugas from the eastern Chukchi Sea population summer in the Beaufort Sea.
- Belugas from the eastern Chukchi Sea population use the near shore Beaufort Sea oil and gas lease areas during summer and autumn.
- Belugas from the eastern Chukchi Sea stock demonstrate age and/or gender related differences in movements and habitat use.

METHODS

Capturing and Tagging of Whales

We attempted to capture belugas beginning in 1996 but were unable to do so in that year, or in 1997 or 2000. In 1996, few belugas were available for capture after the harvest. Ice conditions, weather and/or few animals prevented tagging in 1997 and 2000. We were successful at capturing and tagging whales in 1998, 1999, 2001 and 2002. In each of those years we captured animals during or up to five or six days after the annual subsistence drive hunt. The hunters of Point Lay landed three whales in 1997, 48 in 1998, 33 in 1999, none in 2000, 33 in 2001 and 45 in 2002. In each of these years 10 to 40 belugas remained alive in the lagoon after the hunt. Our capture efforts focused on those remaining animals.

Orr et al. (2001) described three techniques for capturing belugas. We used two of those and one additional technique. We captured one animal using the hoop net technique during the drive hunt in 1998. With this technique, a person jumps from a moving boat and puts a hoop net over a beluga's head as it comes to the surface. The second technique was described by Orr et al. (2001) as an anchored "gill net". They monitored the net while waiting for a beluga to swim into it and become entangled. We modified this second technique slightly. We set an unanchored net (~50 m long, 4 m deep, and with 37.5 cm stretched mesh) across a channel of the lagoon and drove one or two belugas at a time into the net. The third technique we used was to drive belugas into very shallow water, using small boats (usually inflatable) with outboard motors, until the whales could no longer maneuver easily. A person would jump into the water, wade to the whale and place a hoop net over the whale's head. This technique was especially successful in Kasegaluk Lagoon where there is a considerable amount of shallow water. The last technique also minimized danger to the whale and people by eliminating long nets or leaping out of moving boats. In 1999 we also tagged four whales that had become stranded in shallow water during the drive hunt.

After belugas were caught we handled them as described by Orr et al. (2001). We secured whales with a hoop net over their head and flippers. A padded rope was placed around the caudal peduncle and the beluga was slowly pulled to shore. The animals were held in water shallow enough that their dorsum was exposed. They were released immediately after the transmitters were attached. Most belugas that we captured remained in the channels of Kasegaluk Lagoon for 2–5 days after they were tagged with the exception of the one whale we captured with a hoop net. We guided that animal out of the lagoon shortly after tagging. In 1999, we attempted to drive the belugas out of the lagoon but they remained in the deeper channels and would not cross over shallow areas until the water level in the lagoon rose and the belugas left of their own accord.

We used 0.5-watt output satellite data recorders (SDRs) manufactured by Wildlife Computers (Redmond, WA). SDRs deployed in 1998 and 1999 (and one tag in 2001) were ST-10 transmitters, while most of those used in 2001 and 2002 were ST-16 transmitters. In 2002, we also deployed one SPOT2 transmitter (location only). Most SDRs were glued to nylon belting in one of two configurations, saddle mount or side mount (Figure 1). We deployed nine saddle and 9 side mounted tags (Table 1). We also deployed five tags with spider mount configurations (Figure 1, Table 1).

Each saddle mount weighed ~750 gm and measured 14.8 x 10.0 x 3.8 cm. Four C-cell lithium batteries powered the tags. The side mounts weighed ~300 gm and the spider mounts about 330 gm. Side, spider and SPOT tags measured approximately 13 x 5 x 3 cm and were powered with either two 2/3A batteries or 4 M1 (military grade) batteries. The saddle, side and spider tags used a pressure transducer to measure dive depth. All transmitters collected data continuously but a conductivity switch allowed transmissions only when the tag was out of the water. Transmitters were attached with three (for spider mounts) or four (for saddle and side mounts) nylon or dacron pins, approximately 0.33 m long. The pins were inserted through the skin and blubber of the dorsal ridge and fit through pre-cut holes in the belting of each transmitter or through adjustable loops of the spider mounts. Nylon or dacron washers and nuts were screwed onto the pins, which held the transmitter to the back of each animal.

Satellite Tag Data Analysis

Data from the satellite-tagged belugas were obtained from Service ARGOS (see ARGOS, 1988 and Fancy et al., 1988 for a detailed description of the ARGOS data collection and location system). Data included a location for the SDR if sufficient signals were received during a satellite pass, or dive and battery strength data if only one uplink occurred. Service ARGOS assigns a location quality code to each location record that it provides. In our analysis we used all location qualities except class "Z", which consists of those that do not pass ARGOS plausibility tests. ARGOS predicts that locations of quality code 3 are within 150 m of the actual location, code 2 are within 350 m, code 1 are within 1 km, and code 0 are >1 km (ARGOS, 1988), although there is evidence that the locations may not be this accurate in some cases (Burns and Castellini, 1998; Goulet et al., 1999; Vincent et al., 2002).

We screened location records using a computer program that calculated the time, distance, and speed between sequential pairs of locations. The program identified pairs of records that indicated apparent speeds greater than 20 km/hour over periods longer than 10 minutes. The identified records were inspected visually and the ones that appeared erroneous were deleted. The location records used in this paper include only those that remained after the screening process. This screening process was similar to that used by Lowry et al. (1998).

For analysis and presentation, dates and times reported by Service ARGOS were converted from Greenwich mean time to true local time (Alaska Standard Time) by subtracting 11 hours. A computer program calculated the average daily position for each whale based on all records obtained during a 24-hour period, local time.

Data on sea ice coverage were obtained from the National Oceanic and Atmospheric Administration's National Ice Center. Average daily positions for belugas and sea ice coverage maps were displayed and analyzed with the geographic information systems ArcInfo and ArcView.

RESULTS

Capture and Tagging

We captured and tagged 23 belugas near Point Lay in 1998, 1999, 2001 and 2002 (Table 1). In 1998 and 1999, the hunters drove belugas into the lagoon from among the first groups of animals to pass by Kasegaluk Lagoon. These early groups consisted almost entirely of males. In 1998, Point Lay hunters drove belugas into Kasegaluk Lagoon on 26 June. All forty-eight hunted and also the five tagged whales were adult males. In 1999, whales were driven into the lagoon on 30 June. Twenty-eight of thirty-three hunted and four of five tagged animals were adult males. The hunts in 2001 and 2002 occurred later in the season and included many more females and young animals. In 2001, sixteen males and thirteen females were taken in the hunt on 3 July. We tagged five males (three adults and two immature) and three females (one adult and two immature). In 2002, twenty-seven males and eighteen females were taken in the hunt on 7 July. We tagged three males (all immature) and two females (one adult and one immature). In total we tagged twelve adult males, five immature males, two adult females and four immature females. The sixteen male belugas ranged in length from 267 to 441 cm and the seven females from 266 to 368 cm (Table 1).

SDRs provided location information over periods ranging from 5 to 154 days. Two of the tags failed within the first week, another six transmitted for about six weeks and the remaining fifteen lasted about two months or longer. On average, tags transmitted data for 67 days. Saddle mounts averaged 52 days, spider mounts 68 days and side mounts 81 days, although there was no significant difference among longevity of tag types (Kruskal-Wallis: χ^2=1.86, p=0.39). One tag failed because a polar bear (*Ursus maritimus*) killed one of the belugas in 1999 while the whale was still in Kasegaluk Lagoon. We do not know why the other tags failed; however, we suspect most failed because the tag fell off, was rubbed off or the antennae broke when belugas rubbed against ice or the sea floor. In this report we discuss only those tags that operated for more than five days.

Movement Patterns

After capture and tagging in 1998, the animals moved northeast from Kasegaluk Lagoon paralleling the coast toward Point Barrow. There was some movement back toward the southwest but the overall movement was to the northeast. The three males with functioning tags after 15 days traveled due north of Barrow to about 75°N and then moved to the northeast, apparently traveling together (Figure 2). They ceased their northward movement in early August just north of 80°N 134°W and turned to the south after remaining near 80°N for five or six days. After turning south, they separated and used a large extent of the Beaufort Sea at least until the tags ceased sending signals, between late August and mid-October.

In 1999, initial movements of the tagged whales were similar to 1998, they moved northeastward from Kasegaluk Lagoon to the area north of Point Barrow (Figure 3). The immature female (99-2) remained near the shelf break just north of Barrow (near Barrow Canyon) throughout the summer. One of the males (99-1) moved north and east of Point Barrow to approximately 77°N 126°W, then turned south. The two remaining males (99-3 and 99-4) followed almost the exact same northern/northeastern route as was used in 1998. In 1999, the whales turned south at about 79°N after remaining there for approximately four days. Again, the males used a vast amount of the Beaufort Sea during the late summer.

Belugas tagged in 2001 also moved north and east after tagging, from Kasegaluk Lagoon to the area east of Point Barrow (Figure 4). Most of the whales spent July and August along the continental shelf break between Point Barrow and the Canadian border. In July, several animals (01-1, 01-3 and 01-4) moved north into deeper water, to between 73°N and about 75°N, for excursions that lasted 5 to 6 days, but then returned to the shelf break. Two of those animals also moved east, one (01-4) as far northeast as 76°N, 128°W in mid-September. Four tags transmitted data through October, later than in any other year of the study. Those four whales moved southwest from the Beaufort Sea into the Chukchi Sea. They moved a considerable distance to the west through the Chukchi Sea, into Russian waters, before returning to U.S. waters off Alaska. Three of the tags continued sending signals into November and early December. The belugas moved south through the eastern portion of Bering Strait. The last signals were received when the whales were in the Bering Sea north of St. Lawrence Island (Figure 4).

In 2002, the initial movements of belugas differed from other years. Instead of moving northeast toward Point Barrow, the animals tended to move to the west before traveling north (Figure 5). In one case, an immature female (02-1), moved southwest along the coast before turning to the north. She then traveled approximately 900 km to the west before returning east to the shelf break north of Point Barrow. As in 2001, the animals tagged in 2002 tended to stay along the shelf break through the summer. One animal (02-4), in immature male, made an excursion to 76°N that lasted for several days.

Monthly movements were generally similar among years. In June and July, animals tended to move north and east from the Kasegaluk Lagoon area into the northern Chukchi Sea, western and northern Beaufort Sea and Arctic Ocean (Figure 6). In August, belugas used a large extent of the Chukchi and Beaufort seas and portions of the Arctic Ocean (Figure 7). Barrow Canyon (just northeast of Point Barrow) and the shelf break of the Beaufort Sea were used extensively. In September, Barrow Canyon and the Beaufort Sea shelf break were still used, as were portions of the eastern Beaufort Sea (Figure 8). In October and November, whales began their fall migration. They moved west and south through the western Beaufort Sea, the Chukchi Sea and south through the eastern portion of the Bering Strait (Figure 9).

Summer movement patterns differed between sexes. Adult females tended to remain near the continental shelf break (Figure 10) while adult males tended to venture into the deep waters of the northern Beaufort Sea and the Arctic Ocean (Figure 11). This was especially true of the males that were tagged early in the summer in 1998 and 1999. The adult males moved into deep ice-covered waters and remained there for most of the summer. Adult males that were captured from groups that also included adult females also ventured into deep water but apparently for shorter periods of time and not to the same extent as males in 1998 and 1999. Immature females (Figure 10) and males (Figure 11) tended to remain in shallower waters, near the shelf break during the summer, although one female and three males occasionally ventured into deeper waters. One of these northern excursions occurred in late July but the other three occurred in mid- to late September, once the ice had retreated farther to the north.

Distribution Relative to Bathymetry and Ice Cover

Once belugas left the shallow Chukchi Sea, they rarely used the inshore waters of the Beaufort Sea (Figure 12). The shelf break and deep waters of the northern Beaufort Sea and the southern Arctic Ocean were used extensively by many of the tagged whales from July to September. Many of the whales spent a considerable amount of time near Barrow Canyon, approximately 50 km northeast of Point Barrow. They also spent much time along the continental shelf break, both east and west of Barrow Canyon.

Beluga locations along the shelf break occurred in water depths of approximately 200 m and deeper. Whales also occurred frequently in the northern Beaufort Sea and Arctic Ocean during the summer where water depths were up to approximately 4000 m deep.

Ice cover was greater than 90% for many of the beluga locations in late June and early July. For the whales that traveled into the northern Beaufort Sea and Arctic Ocean, ice cover was also frequently 90% or greater. The pack ice retreats to the north during the summer, typically reaching its farthest north retreat in August or early September. In 1998 and 2002, ice retreat was among the greatest ever observed, while 1999 was closer to average, and 2001 was a more severe year. Figures 2 to 5 show ice concentrations in mid-July and early September along with beluga locations throughout the summer in each year. It is unknown how the extent of ice retreat in August and September affected beluga movements; however, movements in June and July did not seem to be limited by ice, as ice covered most of the areas of the Beaufort Sea and northern Chukchi Sea that were used by tagged belugas.

Distribution Relative to the Beaufort Sea Outer Continental Shelf Lease Areas

Use of the lease areas of the Outer Continental Shelf (OCS) of the Beaufort Sea by the belugas that we tagged was confined to the western and northern areas (Figure 13). Only 159 (12.4%) of 1,282 average daily locations were within the OCS lease area (Table 2). Of the locations within the lease area, only 11 (0.9% of the total) were east of 150°W. Most of the remaining locations (n=95; 7.4%) were west of 154°W, mostly off Point Barrow or near Barrow Canyon.

DISCUSSION

Tag attachments and longevity

The attachment technique we used appears to have little long-term impact on beluga whales. Orr et al. (1998) reported recaptures and observations of three belugas previously tagged with SDRs, similar to those we deployed. They speculated, based on scarring patterns, that the nylon pins migrated out of the dorsal ridge leading to release of the transmitter and loss of signals. The three belugas they observed showed no sign of infection or excessive scarring.

In 1999, Point Lay hunters harvested one of the belugas we tagged in 1998 (98-5, Figure 13). This beluga was driven into the lagoon on 26 June in 1998 and on 30 June in 1999. The animal was obviously scarred but with no apparent adverse impacts. The scars appeared to be healed. Based on the scarring pattern on this beluga, it appeared that the pins at the anterior end of the tag had migrated out of the dorsal ridge first followed by the posterior pins at some later date.

Our tag longevity, 5 to 154 days, was similar to that experienced in other studies of beluga whales. In the Canadian High Arctic, Smith and Martin (1994) received signals for <1 to 75 days. Richard et al. (2001a), also in the Canadian High Arctic, had tags last from 1 to 126 days. In the eastern Beaufort Sea, Richard et al. (2001b) had tags that lasted 1 to 129 days with a median tag longevity of 31, 38, and 81 days over three years. Our median tag longevity was more consistent ranging from 60 to 81 days.

The longevity of the tags appears to be limited by the attachment technique and not battery power (Richard et al., 2001a). The nylon pins holding the tag onto the beluga eventually pull out of the blubber and skin of the dorsal ridge and the tag falls off (Orr et al., 1998). To obtain greater tag longevity, a different attachment technique, a modified transmitter size or shape, or both are needed.

Movements and Distribution

Most, if not all belugas, move into shallow coastal or estuarine waters during at least a portion of the summer (Caron and Smith, 1990; Frost and Lowry, 1990). These summer concentration areas are consistently used from year to year and the waters are usually brackish and relatively warm. The reasons for occupying coastal areas are not completely known but may include feeding (Frost et al., 1983; Seaman et al., 1988; Huntington et al., 1999), calving (Sergeant, 1973; Fraker et al., 1979; Brodie et al., 1981), and molting (St. Aubin et al., 1990). Moving into coastal areas may also provide a thermal advantage to adults and particularly neonates (Sergeant and Brodie, 1969; Fraker et al., 1979). Eastern Chukchi Sea belugas move into coastal areas along Kasegaluk Lagoon in late June and animals are sighted in the area until about mid-July (Frost and Lowry, 1990, Frost et al., 1993). The absence of significant stomach contents in belugas killed in the subsistence hunt (Suydam, Frost, and Lowry, unpubl. data) suggests feeding is not the major reason for their presence near Kasegaluk Lagoon. Frost et al. (1993) suggested that belugas likely congregate near Kasegaluk Lagoon to molt. Some of the largest gravel beds along the Chukchi Sea coast are located near the passes into Kasegaluk. Belugas often occur very near shore (sometimes only a few meters from shore) in these areas and stir up bottom sediments, possibly from rubbing to slough off old skin. The low saline and warmer water exiting the lagoons may facilitate the molting process. Belugas with both "old skin" and "new skin" are taken in the Point Lay hunt.

Prior to this study, the movements of eastern Chukchi Sea belugas, after they left the Kasegaluk Lagoon area, were unknown. We expected the belugas to move north from Kasegaluk Lagoon and spend the summer in the northern Chukchi and western Beaufort seas.

Initial movements of the belugas we tagged were as expected. Almost all of the tagged whales moved northeastward from the capture location near Point Lay toward Point Barrow. Frost and Lowry (1990) noted that sightings of belugas along the Chukchi Sea coast tended to occur progressively from south to north. Our results of tagged belugas fit their observations as the belugas generally moved from the south to the north. One of our tagged females was a notable exception. She initially moved south from Point Lay and then traveled a considerable distance to the north and west before returning to the east to near Barrow Canyon. No other tagged whales traveled so far to the west in our study.

Movements of tagged belugas, after the initial northeastward movement, were unexpected in some cases. Males tagged in 1998 and 1999 are the most notable example. During July and August the tagged males traveled far to the north to deep offshore waters (~4000 m deep) with heavy ice cover (>90%). They reached their northernmost locations by late July or early August, similar to whales tagged in the Mackenzie River Delta (Richard et al., 2001b). The use of deep, offshore, and ice-covered habitats during the summer was unexpected. Belugas have traditionally been thought to inhabit shallow, coastal waters in the summer. Other researchers have shown that belugas migrated through deep, offshore habitats during the summer but tended to remain in coastal waters, bays and estuaries, although occasionally animals moved into deep offshore waters (Smith and Martin, 1994; Richard et al., 2001a, b). Our results show that belugas consistently use deep, ice-covered, offshore areas during the summer.

The reasons for the observed movements far to the north are unknown. The movements of the three animals in 1998 and two animals in 1999 were direct and coordinated, possibly indicating prior knowledge of a resource. Belugas may move north to exploit a food resource (Martin and Smith, 1992; Smith and Martin, 1994; Richard et al, 2001b). One such resource, arctic cod (*Boreogadus saida*), can occur in dense patches and is important prey of marine mammals in the Arctic (Frost and Lowry, 1981; Lowry and Frost, 1981; Welch et al., 1993). There are no data on distribution or concentrations of arctic cod or other beluga food items so far north.

Belugas tagged later in the season in other years tended to behave differently than the males in 1998 and 1999. Males and females that were tagged later in the summer, tended to remain near the shelf break for most of the summer. Occasionally animals forayed a considerable distance to the north or east (or west on one occasion). The reasons for these forays are unknown. Richard et al (2001b) observed a similar situation. Animals that were captured early in the season moved to areas that animals captured later in the season did not. Males that were tagged early moved into the deep ice covered waters of Viscount Melville Sound where they appeared to forage (Richard et al., 2001b), whereas males tagged later in the season tended to remain farther to the south and in waters covered with less ice. Richard et al. (2001b) speculated that the later tagged whales remained farther south because of impending formation of ice in the fall or the possibility that prey availability may have been sufficient in the south.

During fall migration, belugas tagged in the eastern Beaufort Sea mostly moved west along the shelf break of the Beaufort Sea, although a small number migrated far north of the shelf break through heavy ice near 75°N (Richard et al., 1997, 1998b, 2001b). Aerial surveys confirm the importance of shelf break habitat for belugas in the Beaufort Sea during fall migration (Moore et al., 2000). The westward fall migration of the eastern Beaufort Sea stock begins in late August to mid-September (Richard et al., 1997, 1998b, 2001b) with whales moving far to the west of Alaska into Russian waters. They may remain near Wrangel Island for weeks before moving south into the Bering Sea (Richard et al., 2001b). Whales occasionally remained in certain areas for periods of days, weeks or even a month, possibly to feed (Richard et al., 1998a).

The whales we tagged in the eastern Chukchi Sea initiated fall migration in October or November, apparently later in the year than eastern Beaufort Sea belugas. If this is true, belugas of the eastern Beaufort Sea would have migrated west along the shelf break passing by whales from the eastern Chukchi Sea. During June, July and part of August it is likely that the ranges of these two stocks did not overlap much. In August and later in the year, eastern Chukchi Sea and eastern Beaufort Sea belugas may occur in similar places and similar times, assuming that the relatively small sample sizes over a few years of tagging are representative of typical movement patterns. The significance of the apparent overlap or the mingling of these two stocks in early fall is uncertain, particularly since studies of mitochondrial DNA clearly indicate the two stocks are genetically discrete (O'Corry-Crowe et al., 1997, 2002).

Gender- and age-related differences in movements

In 1998 and 1999, we tagged mostly large adult males because large adult males were available to be tagged. It is likely that the whales tagged in 1998 and 1999 belonged to one of the first groups to pass Point Lay in those years. Eskimos of Little Diomede Island (cited in Burns and Seaman, 1986) reported that the first groups to pass north during spring migration consisted of large adult males. Other males, females and young migrate later. Based on the sex compositions of the harvests and captures in 1998 and 1999 at Point Lay, it appears that sexual segregation, and possibly age segregation, occurs in the eastern Chukchi Sea stock of belugas.

Movements of males tagged from among those first male groups passing by Point Lay in 1998 and 1999 are considerably different than movements of animals tagged in 2001 and 2002. The 1998–1999 adult males moved much farther north and into much deeper water than the animals tagged from groups that contained more females and young animals. Early season males tagged in the eastern Beaufort Sea also tended to move farther to the north than animals tagged later in the season (Richard et al., 2001b). Richard et al. (2001b) suggested that the later tagged males might have remained farther south due to impending ice formation or distribution of prey resources. We think it unlikely that ice conditions *per se* were responsible for the differing behavior among years in our study. The 1998–1999 males were tagged only 4–9 days earlier than the two males that moved the farthest north in 2001–2002, and one was still north of 80°N in August. Also, the 1998–1999 males moved through hundreds of kilometers of >90% ice cover to reach their northernmost location. Although it is possible that belugas might find prey resources at such northern locations, or alternately not move north because adequate prey are located elsewhere, there are no data to either confirm or reject these possibilities.

In the high Canadian Arctic, the summer range did not differ between males and females (Richard et al., 2001a). Belugas of the high Canadian Arctic occur among the myriad of islands of the Canadian Archipelago. Use of those habitats may differ between males and females but not on a scale that is detectable with satellite telemetry. Shallow and deepwater habitats occur in close proximity in the Canadian Archipelago. Males may be using some of those deep-water habitats differently than females.

Shallow water and deep-water habitats are farther apart in the Beaufort and Chukchi seas than in the Canadian high Arctic. Movement patterns of eastern Chukchi and Beaufort Sea belugas were more similar to each other than to those in the high Canadian Arctic. Males from both stocks tended to move to different locations than females and occupy different habitats. In this study, adult males moved farther north than subadult males and all belugas that moved north of 75°N were males. Males tagged in the Mackenzie River Delta spent little time in the delta and also traveled north to areas of heavy ice cover, while females remained mostly near shore and in relatively shallow water (Richard et al., 1997, 1998b). Unlike females in the Mackenzie, Chukchi Sea females were seldom found in water shallower than 200 m during summer.

The behavior of the eastern Chukchi Sea stock of belugas seems to parallel that of another but much larger odontocete, the sperm whale (*Physeter catodon*). Large sperm whale males tend to occur at higher latitudes than females and immature animals except during mating when large males will accompany females groups (Whitehead, 1993). Males are larger than females in both sperm whales and belugas. The larger body sizes of male belugas may enable them to deal better with ice-covered waters than females and young (Martin and Smith, 1999). Larger animals should be able to dive deeper and longer than smaller ones, thus providing more security for finding openings in the ice for breathing and for accessing prey resources.

Movements in relation to ice and bathymetry

Ice influences the movements and distribution of marine mammals, including beluga whales (Fay, 1974). Belugas are frequently associated with sea ice (Frost and Lowry, 1990; Moore et al., 2000). The association with ice was typically thought to be weakest in summer (Hazard, 1988). This perception was probably due to the limited ability to collect data. Observing belugas in broken ice or ice-cover greater than 90% is difficult, at best. The use of satellite telemetry has allowed new insights into beluga's association with and penetration of pack ice.

Some of the belugas we tagged penetrated deep into the pack ice of the northern Beaufort Sea and southern Arctic Ocean. Belugas tagged in the eastern Beaufort Sea also penetrated deep into the ice, especially between the islands of northwest Canada (Richard et al., 2001b). In both these studies, ice-cover was often greater than 90%; however, during summer the ice is frequently in motion and cracks form as the ice shifts. Additionally, the relatively warm summer temperatures dictate that open water does not freeze quickly. Movement of the ice in combination with warm temperatures should allow belugas to easily find breathing holes in the pack ice, and in fact the movements of the belugas tagged in these two studies strongly suggest that ice-cover in the Beaufort Sea and Arctic Ocean does not limit beluga movements during the summer.

Other stocks of belugas may be more restricted by ice. In the high Canadian Arctic, ice between islands blocks movements of belugas (Smith and Martin, 1994; Richard et al., 2001a). Ice between islands and in fjords is likely different from ice in an ocean basin. On the ocean, ice is frequently in motion. As the ice moves, cracks, leads or polynyas form, providing belugas access to the ocean surface to breath. Ice between islands or in fjords likely does not move or shift as readily as ice on the open ocean. Therefore, there may be a greater risk of entrapment to belugas that penetrate ice in narrow passages between landmasses than on the open ocean. Entrapments have occurred in areas other than between islands or in fjords, but only when rapid extreme freezing conditions exist (e.g. air temperatures are very low and the there is no wind) (Burns and Seaman, 1986; Siegstad and Heide-Jørgenson, 1994). When the sea surface freezes quickly and ice becomes stationary, belugas may become entrapped and are easily hunted or preyed upon by polar bears (*Ursus maritimus*) (Burns and Seaman, 1986; Lowry et al., 1987; Siegstad and Heide-Jørgenson, 1994; Heide-Jørgenson et al., 2002). It is obvious that ice generally did not restrict movements of the belugas we tracked in the Arctic Ocean during the summer.

Information from tagging studies has dramatically changed our understanding of habitat use, distribution and movements of belugas. For example, prior to satellite tagging efforts, eastern Beaufort Sea belugas were presumed to spend the summer in relatively nearshore Beaufort Sea waters of Amundsen Gulf and the Mackenzie Estuary. They were thought to be relatively shallow divers and primarily pelagic, mid-water feeders. It is now clear that many of the belugas tagged in the eastern Beaufort Sea and the eastern Chukchi Sea do not remain in shallow, nearshore waters but travel hundreds of kilometers to the north through heavy pack ice, presumably to feed. They often dive to depths exceeding 400 m (Martin et al., 1998; Martin and Smith, 1999; unpubl. data, this study). Those that do not travel into deep, ice covered waters remain near the shelf break, which is approximately 50 to 100 km north of the coast of Alaska and make dives of 100–300 m.

Use of the Beaufort Sea Outer Continental Shelf Lease Sale Area

Evaluation of potential impacts from oil and gas activities in the Beaufort Sea has focused on bowhead whales and belugas from the eastern Beaufort Sea stock. Eastern Beaufort Sea stock belugas migrate east through the Beaufort Sea in April and May and return west in late August through October (Richard et al., 2001b) and thus may be exposed to industrial activities in the Beaufort Sea. Satellite tracking of eastern Chukchi Sea belugas has revealed that this stock also spends a portion of the summer in the Beaufort Sea (this study; Suydam et al., 2001). Those whales moved north along the Chukchi Sea coast of northwestern Alaska and into the Beaufort Sea. The animals spent most of the summer along the shelf break of the Beaufort Sea and the northeastern Chukchi Sea or farther to the north. They did not commonly use the nearshore shelf within the OCS lease area.

Movements of belugas tagged in the eastern Beaufort Sea (Richard et al., 2001b), the eastern Chukchi Sea (this study) and those observed during aerial surveys in the Beaufort Sea (Moore et al., 2000), show that the shelf break of the Beaufort Sea is important to belugas. The reasons why belugas occur here so frequently are unknown, but could be related to upwelling seawater that concentrates prey. Belugas infrequently used nearshore habitats in the central Beaufort Sea, although there were considerable numbers of locations and sightings in the nearshore of the western Beaufort Sea, especially near Barrow Canyon.

ACKNOWLEDGMENTS

This project would not have happened without the contributions and support of multiple people and organizations. Minerals Management Service, through the Coastal Marine Institute at the University of Alaska Fairbanks, and the National Oceanic and Atmospheric Administration provided major funding to the Alaska Beluga Whale Committee through various grants. Funding and in-kind support were also provided by the Village of Point Lay, the North Slope Borough's Department of Wildlife Management, Grants Division and School District, the National Marine Mammal Laboratory of the National Marine Fisheries Service, Commander Northwest, the Alaska Department of Fish and Game, the University of Alaska Fairbanks, and the Washington Fish and Wildlife Cooperative Research Unit at the School of Aquatic and Fishery Sciences at University of Washington.

This project would not have been possible without the help and cooperation of the people and hunters of Point Lay. They invited us into their village to live and work, they allowed us to tag in conjunction with their hunt, and they shared their knowledge about belugas in this area. We especially thank Warren and Dorcus Neakok, Ben Neakok, Bill and Marie Tracey, Gordon Upicksoun, Thomas Nukapigak, Amos Agnasagga, Julius Rexford and Danny Pikok. Many thanks to Charles Aniskette, Alvin Ashby, Vince Dollarhide, Leo Ferreira III, Nick Hank, Lauren Hansen, Rod Hobbs, Laura Litzky, Thomas Nukapigak, Greg O'Corry-Crowe, Jack Orr, Lori Quakenbush, Todd Robeck, Tracy Romano, Bob Small, Heather Smith, Michelle Sparck, Suzann Speckman, Danny Susook, Jim Tazruk, and Glenn and Kris VanBlaricom for assisting with capturing and tagging. Logistical support in Point Lay was provided by Bill and Marie Tracey, Jack Talyor, Jerry Edwards, Julius Rexford and Danny Susook and in Barrow by Dave Ramey and Benny Achootchook. Additional support was received from Douglas DeMaster, Thomas F. Albert, Charles D.N. Brower, Dolores Vinas, Liza Delarosa, April Brower, and John Bengston. Gay Sheffield helped with analysis and presentation of SDR location data. Janice Waite assisted with permit requirements.

STUDY PRODUCTS

2000   Frost, K.J., L.F. Lowry and R. Suydam. Satellite tracking of eastern Chukchi Sea beluga whales in the Beaufort Sea and Arctic Ocean. *In* University of Alaska Coastal Marine Institute. Annual Reports. Fairbanks, AK, University of Alaska, Coastal Marine Institute and USDOI, MMS, Alaska OCS Region.

2001   Frost, K.J., L.F. Lowry and R. Suydam. Satellite tracking of eastern Chukchi Sea beluga whales in the Beaufort Sea and Arctic Ocean. *In* University of Alaska Coastal Marine Institute. Annual Reports. Fairbanks, AK, University of Alaska, Coastal Marine Institute and USDOI, MMS, Alaska OCS Region.

2001   Frost, K.J., L.F. Lowry and R. Suydam. Satellite tracking of eastern Chukchi Sea beluga whales in the Beaufort Sea and Arctic Ocean. Univ. Alaska Coastal Marine Institute Annual Research Review, Fairbanks, AK. Feb. 2001 (abstr.)

2001   Suydam, R., L.F. Lowry and K.J. Frost. Satellite tracking of beluga whales in the central Arctic Ocean. *In* Alaska OCS Region 8th Information Transfer Meeting Proceedings, Preparer MBC Applied Environmental Sciences Anchorage: USDOI, MMS, Alaska OCS Region.

2002   Frost, K.J., L.F. Lowry and R. Suydam. Satellite tracking of eastern Chukchi Sea beluga whales in the Beaufort Sea and Arctic Ocean. *In* University of Alaska Coastal Marine Institute. Annual Reports. Fairbanks, AK, University of Alaska, Coastal Marine Institute and USDOI, MMS, Alaska OCS Region.

2002   Suydam, R., K.J. Frost and L.F. Lowry. Satellite tracking of eastern Chukchi Sea beluga whales in the Beaufort Sea and Arctic Ocean. Univ. Alaska Coastal Marine Institute Annual Research Review, Fairbanks, AK, Feb. 2002 (abstr.)

2003   Suydam, R., K.J. Frost and L.F. Lowry. Satellite tracking of eastern Chukchi Sea beluga whales in the Beaufort Sea and Arctic Ocean. Univ. Alaska Coastal Marine Institute Annual Research Review, Fairbanks, AK, 19 Feb. 2003 (abstr.)

2003   Suydam, R. Satellite tracking of eastern Chukchi Sea beluga whales in the Beaufort Sea and Arctic Ocean. *In* Alaska OCS Region 9th Information Transfer Meeting Proceedings, Preparer MBC Applied Environmental Sciences Anchorage: USDOI, MMS, Alaska OCS Region.

2003   Suydam, R., L. Lowry, K. Frost, G. O'Corry-Crowe and G. VanBlaricom. Satellite tracking of eastern Chukchi Sea beluga whales in the Beaufort Sea and Arctic Ocean, 1998–2002. 15th Conf. Biology of Marine Mammals, 14–19 December 2003 (abstr. and presented paper).

REFERENCES

ARGOS. 1988. Users' manual. Version 1. Toulouse, France: CLS ARGOS.

Brodie, P.F., J.L. Parsons, and D.E. Sergeant. 1981. Present status of the white whale (Delphinapterus leucas) in Cumberland Sound, Baffin Island. Report to the International Whaling Commission 32:579–582.

Burns, J.M. and M.A. Castellini. 1998. Dive data from satellite tags and time-depth recorders: a comparison in Weddell Seal pups. Marine Mammal Science 14:750–764.

Burns, J.J. and G.A. Seaman. 1986. Investigation of belukha whales in coastal waters of western and northern Alaska. II. Biology and Ecology. Final report submitted to MMS and NOAA, Outer Continental Shelf Environmental Assessment Program.

Caron, L.M.J. and T.G. Smith. 1990. Philopatry and site tenacity of belugas, Delphinapterus leucas, hunted by the Inuit at the Nastapoka estuary, eastern Hudson Bay. *In*: Smith, T.G., St. Aubin, D.J., and Geraci, J.R. (eds.). Advances in research on the beluga whale, *Delphinapterus leucas*. Canadian Bulletin of Fisheries and Aquatic Sciences 224. 69–79.

Fancy, S.C., L.F. Pank, D.C. Douglas, C.H. Curby, G.W. Garner, S.C. Amstrup, and W.L. Regilin. 1988. Satellite telemetry: a new tool for wildlife research and management. U.S. Fish and Wildlife Service Resource Publication No. 172. 54pp. U.S. Fish and Wildlife Service, Anchorage, Alaska.

Fay, F.H. 1974. The role of ice in the ecology of marine mammals of the Bering Sea. Pages 383–399 in D.W. Hood and E.J. Kelley (eds.), Oceanography of the Bering Sea. Occ. Publ. No. 2. Inst. Mar. Sci. Univ. Alaska, Fairbanks. 623 p.

Fraker, M.A., C.D. Gordon, J.W. McDonald, J.K.B. Ford, and G. Cambers. 1979. White whale (*Delphinapterus leucas*) distribution and abundance and the relationship to physical and chemical characteristics of the Mackenzie Estuary. Canadian Fisheries and Marine Services Technical Report 863. 59 pp.

Frost, K.J., and L.F. Lowry. 1981. Trophic importance of some marine gadids in northern Alaska and their body-otolith size relationships. Fish. Bull. 79:187–192.

Frost, K.J., and Lowry, L.F. 1990. Distribution, abundance, and movements of beluga whales, Delphinapterus leucas, in coastal waters of western Alaska. *In*: Smith, T.G., St. Aubin, D.J., and Geraci, J.R. (eds.). Advances in research on the beluga whale, *Delphinapterus leucas*. Canadian Bulletin of Fisheries and Aquatic Sciences 224. 39–57.

Frost, K.J., Lowry, L.F., and J.J. Burns. 1983. Distribution of marine mammals in the coastal zone of the eastern Chukchi Sea during summer and autumn. U.S. Department of Commerce, NOAA, OCSEAP Final Report 20:563–650. National Oceanic and Atmospheric Administration, Anchorage, Alaska.

Frost, K.J., Lowry, L.F., and Nelson, R.R.. 1985. Radiotagging studies of beluga whales (*Delphinapterus leucas*) in Bristol Bay, Alaska. Marine Mammal Science 1:191–202.

Frost, K.J., Lowry, L.F., and G. Carroll. 1993. Beluga whale and spotted seal use of a coastal lagoon system in the northeastern Chukchi Sea. Arctic 46:8–16.

Goulet, A.M., M.O. Hammill, and C. Barrette. 1999. Quality of satellite telemetry locations of gray seals (*Halichoerus grypus*). Marine Mammal Science 15:589–594.

Hazard, K. 1988. Beluga whale, *Delphinapterus leucas*. *In*: Lentfer, J.W. Selected marine mammals of Alaska. Marine Mammal Commission, Washington, DC.

Heide-Jørgensen, M.P., P. Richard, M. Ramsay, and S. Akeeagok. 2002. Three recent ice entrapments of Arctic cetaceans in Westr Greenland and the eastern Canadian High Arctic. Pages 143–148. *In*: M.P. Heide-Jørgensen and O. Wiig (eds.) NAMMCO Scientific Publications 4. Tromsø, Norway.

Huntington, H.P. and the Communities of Buckland, Elim, Koyuk, Point Lay, and Shaktoolik. 1999. Traditional knowledge of the ecology of beluga whales (*Delphinapterus leucas*) in the eastern Chukchi and northern Bering seas, Alaska. Arctic 52:49–61.

Lowry, L.F., and K.J. Frost. 1981. Distribution, growth, and foods of arctic cod (<u>*Boreogadus*</u> <u>*saida*</u>) in the Bering, Chukchi, and Beaufort seas. Canadian Field-Naturalist 95:186–191.

Lowry, L.F., and K.J. Frost. 1998. Alaska Beluga Whale Committee surveys of beluga whales in Bristol Bay, Alaska, 1993–1994. Report to the International Whaling Commission's Scientific Committee SC/51/SM32. 13 p.

Lowry, L.F., J.J. Burns, and R.R. Nelson. 1987. Polar bear, *Ursus maritimus*, predation on belugas, *Delphinapterus leucas*, in the Bering and Chukchi seas. Canadian Field-Naturalist 101:141–146.

Lowry, L.F., K.J. Frost, R. Davis, D.P. DeMaster, and R.S. Suydam. 1998. Movements and behavior of satellite-tagged spotted seals (*Phoca largha*) in the Bering and Chukchi Seas. Polar Biology 19:221–230.

Lowry, L.F., D.P. DeMaster, and K.J. Frost. 1999a. Alaska Beluga Whale Committee surveys of beluga whales in the eastern Bering Sea, 1992–1995. Report to the International Whaling Commission's Scientific Committee SC/51/SM34. 22 pp.

Lowry, L.F., D.P. DeMaster, K.J. Frost, and W. Perryman. 1999b. Alaska Beluga Whale Committee surveys of beluga whales in the eastern Chukchi Sea, 1996–1998. Report to the International Whaling Commission's Scientific Committee SC/51/SM33. 20 pp.

Lydersen, C., A.R. Martin, K.M. Kovacs and I. Gjertz. 2001. Summer and autumn movements of white whales *Delphinapterus leucas* in Svalbard, Norway. Marine Ecological Progress Series 219:265–274.

Martin, A.R. and Smith. T.G. 1992. Deep diving in wild, free-ranging beluga whales, *Delphinapterus leucas*. Canadian Journal of Fisheries and Aquatic Sciences 49:462–466.

Martin, A.R. and Smith. T.G. 1999. Strategy and capability of wild belugas, *Delphinapterus leucas*, during deep, benthic diving. Canadian Journal of Zoology 77:1783–1793.

Martin, A.R., T.G. Smith and O.P. Cox. 1993. Studying the behaviour and movements of high arctic belugas with satellite telemetry. Symposia of the Zoological Society of London 66:195–210.

Martin, A.R., T.G. Smith and O.P. Cox. 1998. Dive form and function in belugas *Delphinapterus leucas* of the eastern Canadian High Arctic. Polar Biology 20:218–228.

Moore, S.E., D.P. DeMaster, and P.K. Dayton. 2000. Cetacean habitat selection in the Alaskan Arctic during summer and autumn. Arctic 53:432–447.

Neakok, W., D. Neakok, W. Bodfish, D. Libbey, E.S. Hall Jr., and the Point Lay Elders. 1985. The keep the past alive: the Point Lay cultural resource site survey. 109 pp. North Slope Borough, Barrow, Alaska.

O'Corry-Crowe, G.M., R.S. Suydam, A. Rosenberg, K.J. Frost and A.E. Dizon. 1997. Phylogeography, population structure and dispersal patterns of the beluga whale *Delphinapterus leucas* in the western Nearctic revealed by mitochondrial DNA. Molecular Ecology 6:955–970.

O'Corry-Crowe, G.M., A.E. Dizon, R.S. Suydam and L.F. Lowry. 2002. Molecular genetic studies of population structure and movement patterns in a migratory species: the beluga whales (*Delphinapterus leucas*). Pages 53–64. *In*: C.J. Pfeiffer (ed.). Molecular and Cell Biology of Marine Mammals. Kreiger Publishing Company, Malabar, Florida.

Orr, J., D.J. St. Aubin, P.R. Richard, and M.P. Heide-Jorgensen. 1998. Recapture of belugas, *Delphinapterus leucas*, tagged in the Canadian Arctic. Marine Mammal Science 14:829–834.

Orr, J.R., R. Joe, and D. Evic. 2001. Capturing and handling of white whales (*Delphinapterus leucas*) in the Canadian Arctic for instrumentation and release. Arctic 54:299–304.

Reeves, R.R. and D.J. St. Aubin. 2001. Belugas and narwhals: application of new technology to whale science in the Arctic. Arctic 54:iii-vi.

Richard, P.R., A.R. Martin, and J.R. Orr. 1997. Study of summer and fall movements and dive behavior of Beaufort Sea belugas, using satellite telemetry: 1992–1995. Environmental Studies Research Funds Report No. 134. 26 p.

Richard, P.R., M.P. Heide-Jorgensen and D. St. Aubin. 1998a. Fall movements of belugas (*Delphinapterus leucas*) with satellite-linked transmitters in Lancaster Sound, Jones Sound, and northern Baffin Bay. Arctic 51:5–16.

Richard, P.R., A.R. Martin, and J.R. Orr. 1998b. Study of late summer and fall movements and dive behavior of Beaufort Sea belugas, using satellite telemetry: 1997. Final Report Minerals Management Service OCS Study 98-0016. 25 p.

Richard, P.R., M.P. Heide-Jorgensen, J.R. Orr, R. Dietz and T.G. Smith. 2001a. Summer and autumn movements and habitat use by belugas in the Canadian High Arctic and adjacent areas. Arctic 54:207–222.

Richard, P.R., A.R. Martin and J.R. Orr. 2001b. Summer and autumn movements of belugas of the Eastern Beaufort Sea stock. Arctic 54:223–236.

Seaman, G.A., K.J. Frost and L.F. Lowry. 1982. Foods of belukha whales (*Delphinapterus leucas*) in western Alaska. Cetology 44:1–19.

Seaman, G.A., K.J. Frost and L.F. Lowry. 1988. Investigations of belukha whales in coastal waters of western and northern Alaska. Part I. Distribution and abundance. U. S. Department of Commerce, NOAA, OCSEAP Final Report 56:153–220.

Sergeant, D.E. 1973. Biology of white whales (Delphinapterus leucas) in western Hudson Bay. Journal of the Fisheries Research Board Canada 32:1065–1090.

Sergeant, D.E. and P.F. Brodie. 1969. Body size in white whales, *Delphinapterus leucas*. Journal of the Fisheries Research Board Canada 26:2561–2580.

Siegstad, H. and M.P. Heide-Jørgensen. 1994. Ice entrapments of narwhals (*Monodon monoceros*) and white whales (*Delphinapterus leucas*) in Greenland. Meddelelser om Grønland. Bioscience 39:151–160.

Smith, T.G., and A.R. Martin. 1994. Distribution and movements of belugas, *Delphinapterus leucas*, in the Canadian high arctic. Canadian Journal of Fisheries and Aquatic Sciences 51:1653–1663.

St. Aubin, D.J., T.G. Smith, and J.R. Geraci. 1990. Seasonal epidermal molt in beluga whales, *Delphinapterus leucas*. Canadian Journal of Zoology 68:359–367.

Suydam, R.S., L.F. Lowry, K.J. Frost, G.M. O'Corry-Crowe, and D. Pikok, Jr. 2001. Satellite tracking of eastern Chukchi Sea beluga whales into the Arctic Ocean. Arctic 54:237–243.

Vincent, C., B.J. McConnell, V. Ridoux, and M.A. Fedak. 2002. Assessment of Argos location accuracy from satellite tags deployed on captive gray seals. Marine Mammal Science 18:156–166.

Welch, H.E., R.E. Crawford, and H. Hop. 1993. Occurrence of arctic cod (*Boreogadus saida*) schools and their vulnerability to predation in the Canadian High Arctic. Arctic 46:331–339.

Whitehead, H. 1993. The behaviour of mature male sperm whales on the Galapagos Islands breeding grounds. Canadian Journal of Zoology 71:689–699.

Table 1. Beluga whales instrumented with tags at Point Lay, Alaska in 1998, 1999, 2001 and 2002.

ID Number	Capture Date	Sex	Age class	Color	Length (cm)	PTTID	PTT Type	Last Date	Tag Duration (days)[1]
1998									
98-1	26 June	Male	Adult	White	440	11035	Saddle	8 July	13
98-2	28 June	Male	Adult	White	432	2284	Saddle	12 July	15
98-3	29 June	Male	Adult	White	398	11036	Saddle	10 October	104
98-4	29 June	Male	Adult	White	415	2285	Saddle	28 September	92
98-5	1 July	Male	Adult	White	414	2282	Saddle	29 August	60
1999									
99-1	30 June	Male	Adult	White	418	11035	Side mount	24 September	87
99-2	30 June	Female	Imm.[2]	Gray	266	11036	Side mount	18 September	81
99-3	30 June	Male	Adult	White	424	11037	Saddle	25 August	57
------	30 June	Male	Adult	White	441	11039	Saddle	4 July	5
99-4	30 June	Male	Adult	White	424	11041	Saddle	22 September	85
2001									
01-1	3 July	Male	Adult	White	381	2093	Spider	9 August	38
01-2	3 July	Female	Adult	White	359	2094	Spider	21 July	19
01-3	5 July	Female	Imm.	Gray	316	11038	Side mount	28 November	147
01-4	5 July	Male	Imm.	Gray	324	11041	Side mount	5 December	154
01-5	5 July	Female	Imm.	Gray	335	2280	Side mount	22 October	110
01-6	7 July	Male	Adult	White	340	11037	Spider	16 November	133
01-7	7 July	Male	Imm.	Lt. Gray	320	2281	Side mount	23 July	17
01-8	7 July	Male	Adult	White	373	2282	Saddle	12 August	37
2002									
02-1	7 July	Female	Imm.	Gray	320	11036	Spider	13 September	69
------	7 July	Female	Adult	White	368	11042	Side mount	11 July	5
02-2	7 July	Male	Imm.	Gray	276	11044	Spider	29 September	85
02-3	7 July	Male	Imm.	Gray	274	2090	Side /SPOT	5 September	61
02-4	8 July	Male	Imm.	Gray	267	2088	Side mount	12 September	67

[1] Tag duration = the number of days from when the tag was attached to the beluga to the last day we received a good location that passed data screening.

[2] Imm. = beluga that we classified as immature based on its color.

34

Table 2. Number of average daily locations of satellite tagged belugas within the Beaufort Sea OCS lease sale area, by longitude.

Longitude range	# of beluga locations in OCS area
143–144	0
144–145	0
145–146	1
146–147	0
147–148	3
148–149	4
149–150	3
150–151	6
151–152	10
152–153	21
153–154	16
154–155	43
155–156	52
Total number of locations	159

Figure 1. Configurations of satellite data recorders deployed on beluga whales in the eastern Chukchi Sea in 1998, 1999, 2001 and 2002. Upper panel: saddle tag. Middle panel: side mount. Lower panel: spider tag.

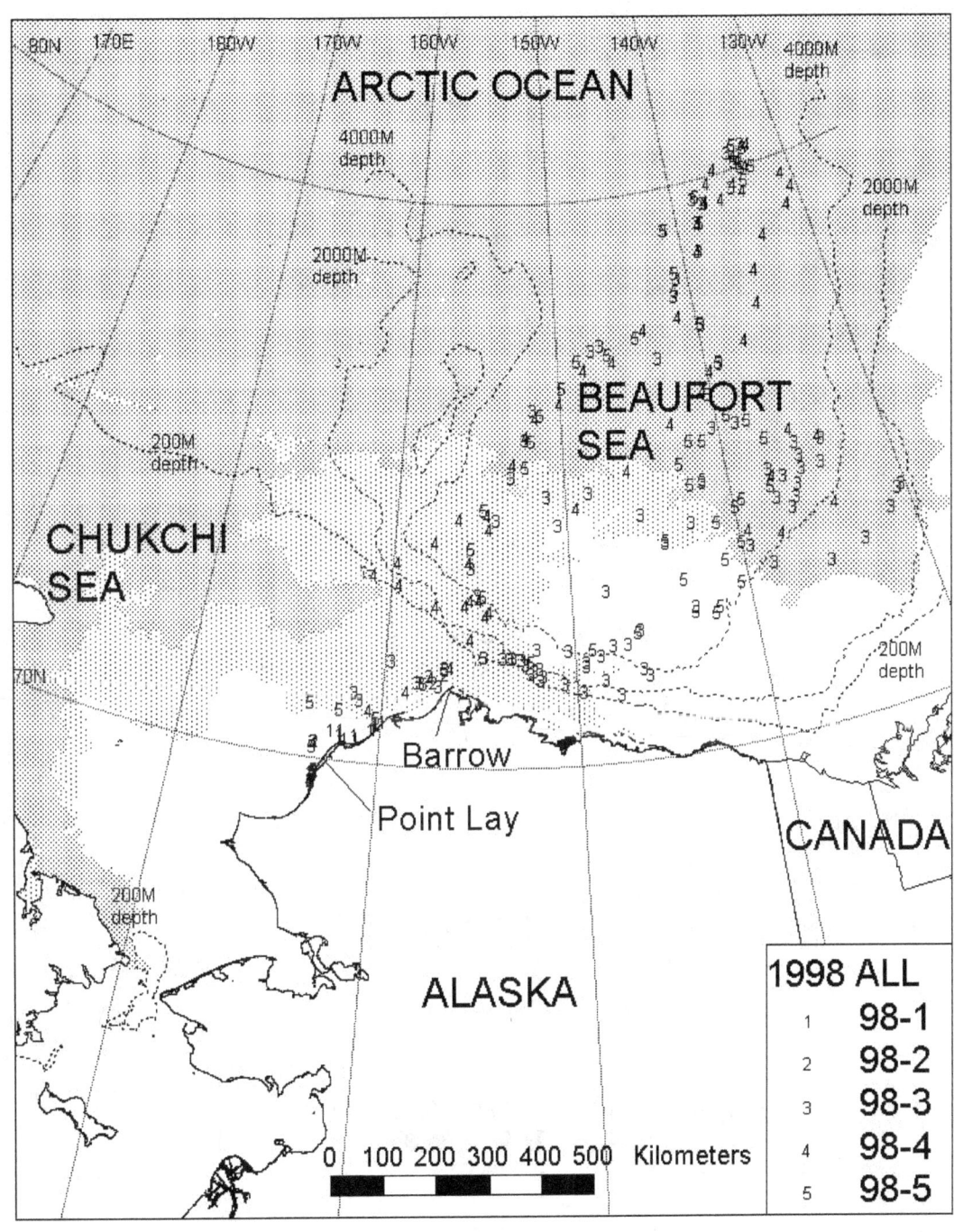

Figure 2. Locations of beluga whales satellite tagged at Point Lay, Alaska, 8 July–10 October 1998. Light stippling is >=30% ice cover on 16 July, dark stippling is >=30% ice cover on 4 September.

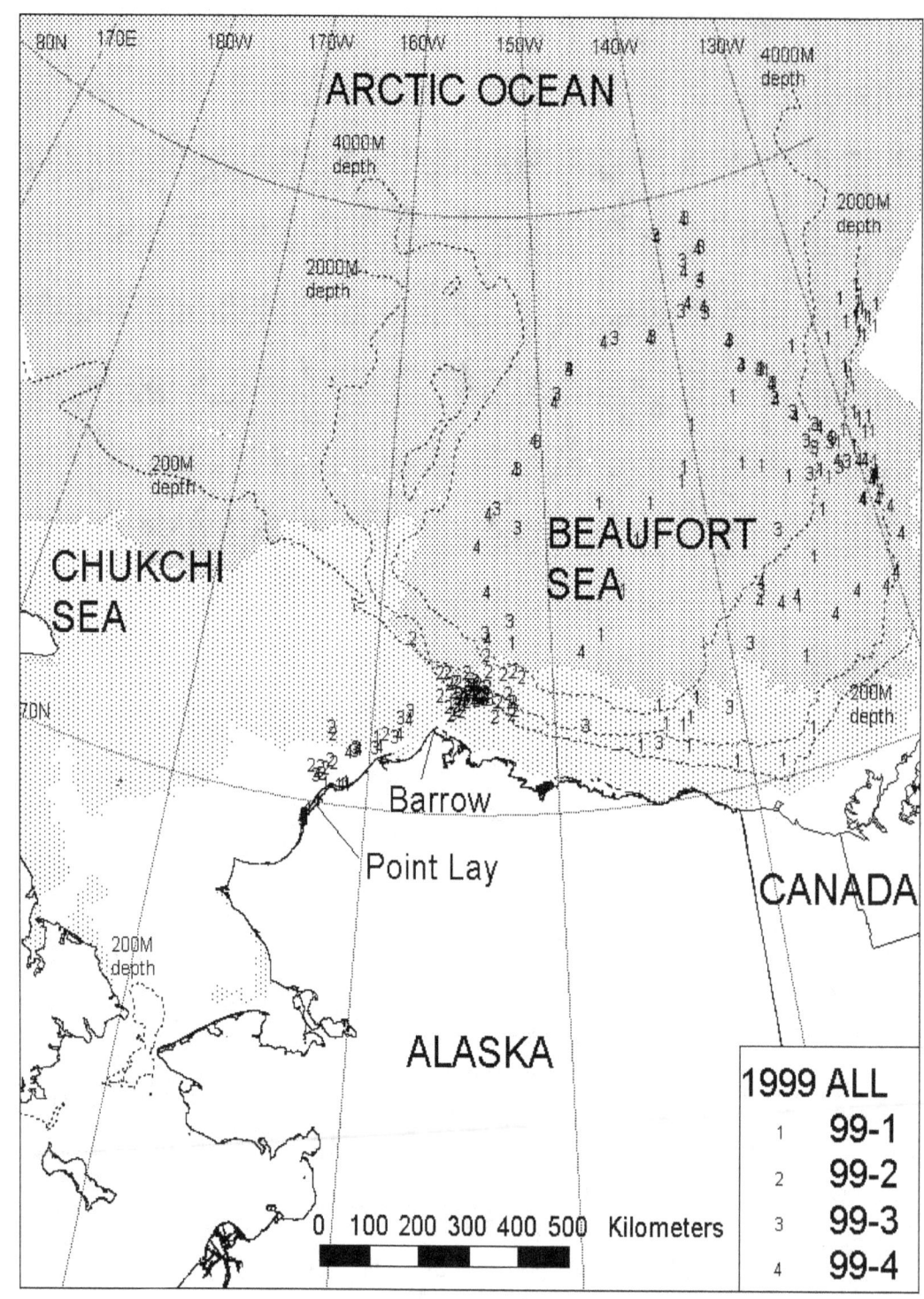

Figure 3. Locations of beluga whales satellite tagged at Point Lay, Alaska, 30 June–24 September 1999. Light stippling is >=30% ice cover on 16 July, dark stippling is >=30% ice cover on 4 September.

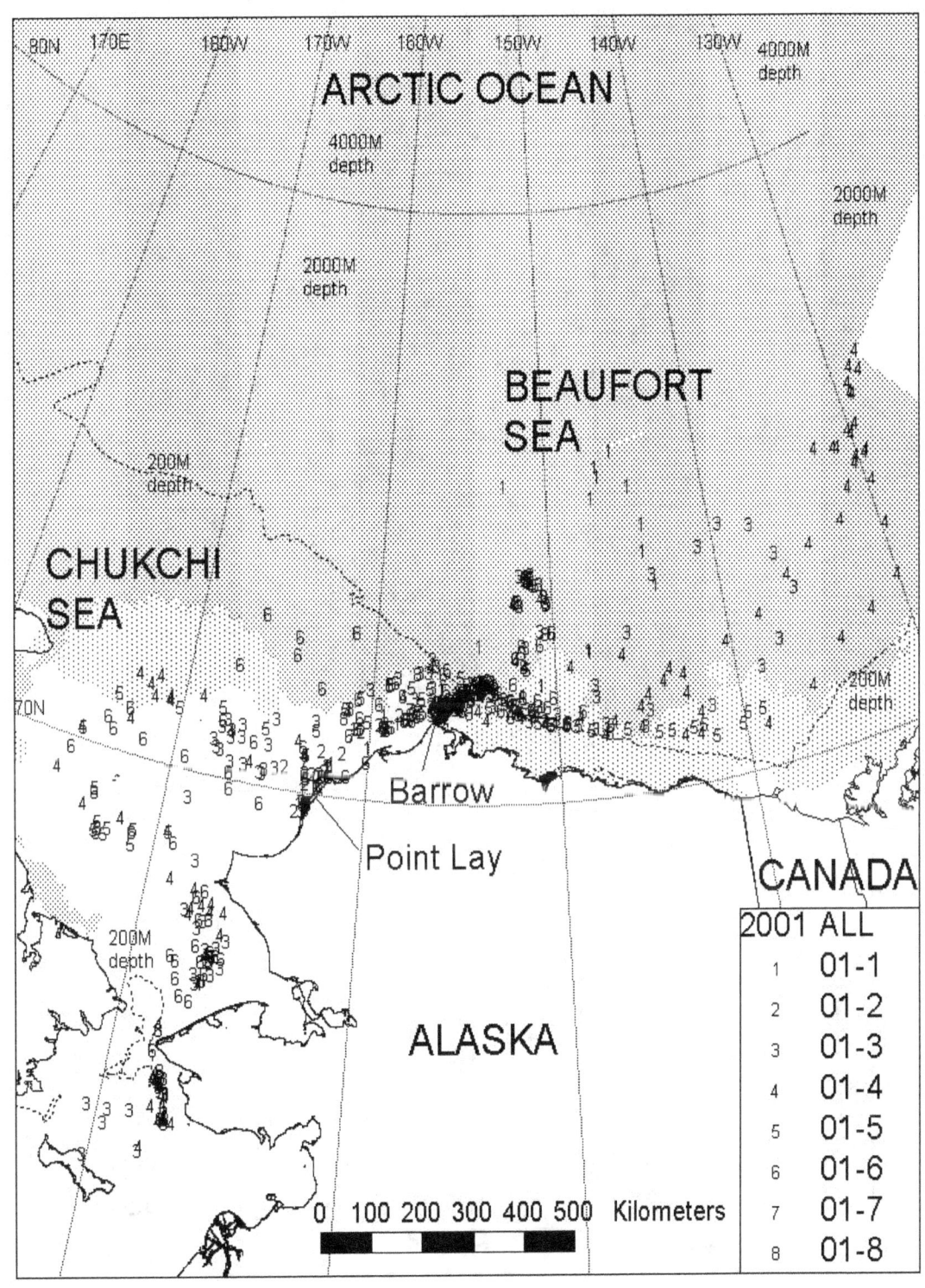

Figure 4. Locations of beluga whales satellite tagged at Point Lay, Alaska, 3 July–5 December 2001. Light stippling is >=30% ice cover on 13 July, dark stippling is >=30% ice cover on 10 September.

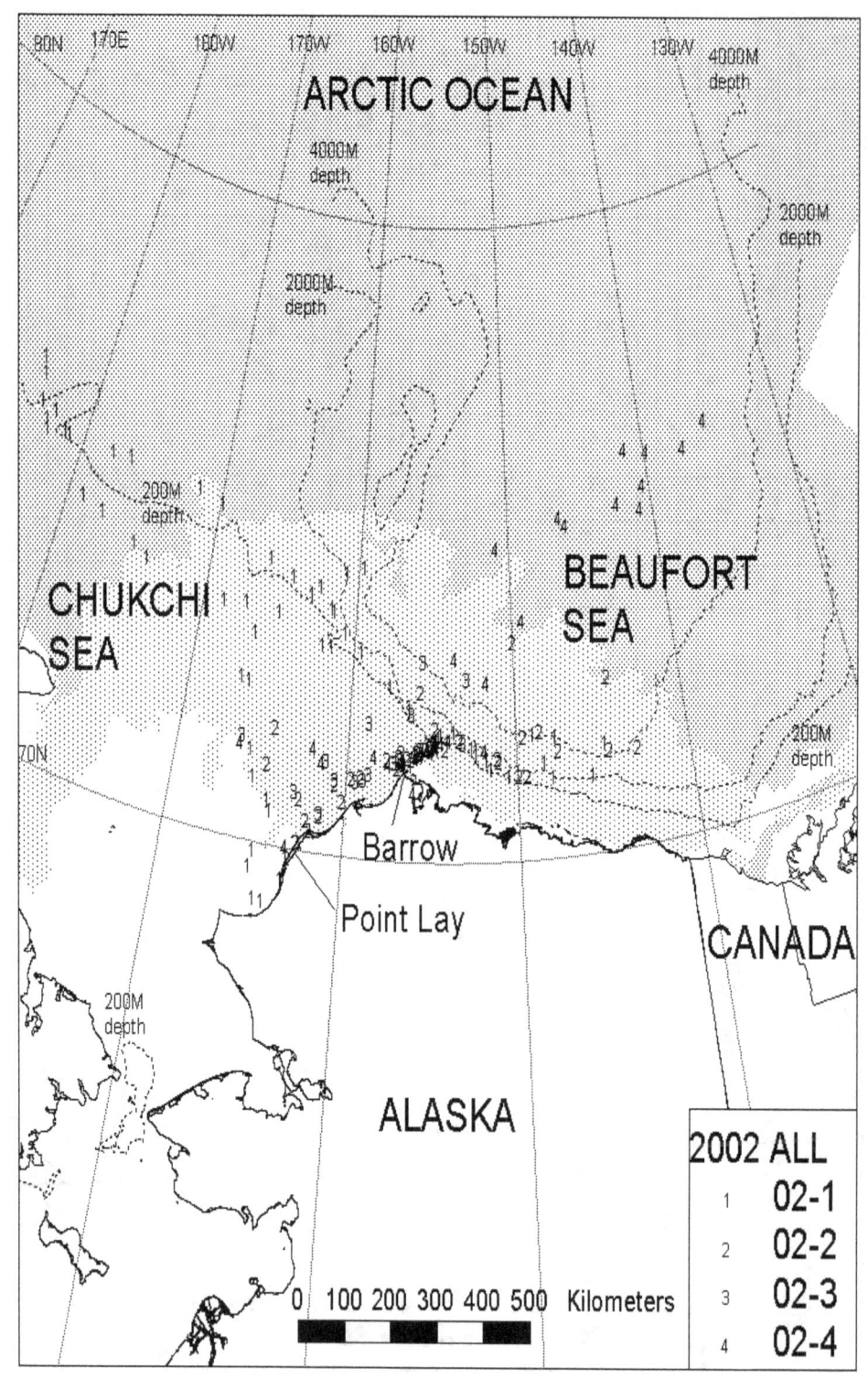

Figure 5. Locations of beluga whales satellite tagged at Point Lay, Alaska, 7 July–29 September 2002. Light stippling is >=30% ice cover on 15 July, dark stippling is >=30% ice cover on 2 September.

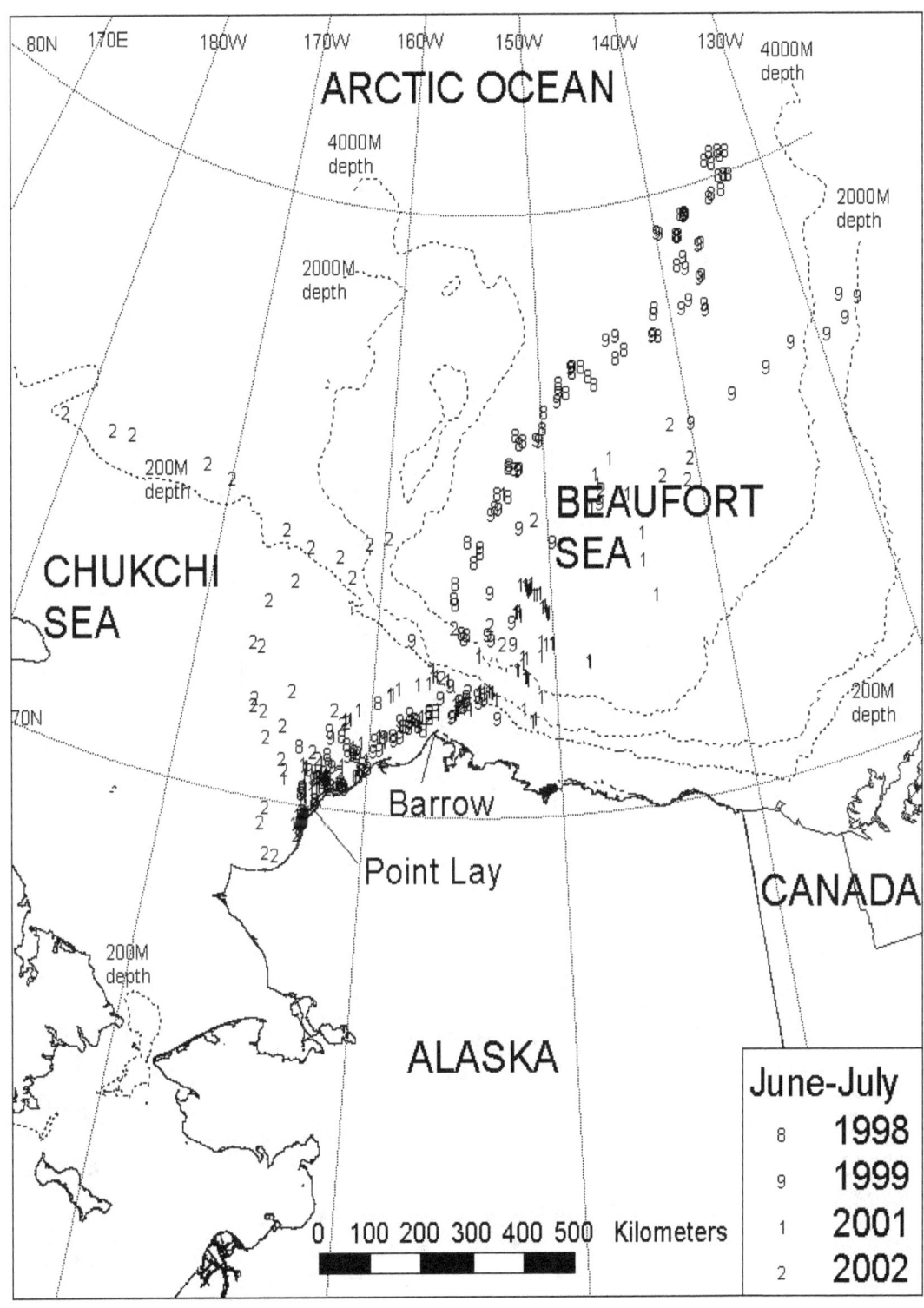

Figure 6. Locations of beluga whales satellite tagged at Point Lay, Alaska, in June and July 1998–2002. (Each number represents a beluga location; locations for all belugas from each respective year are plotted.)

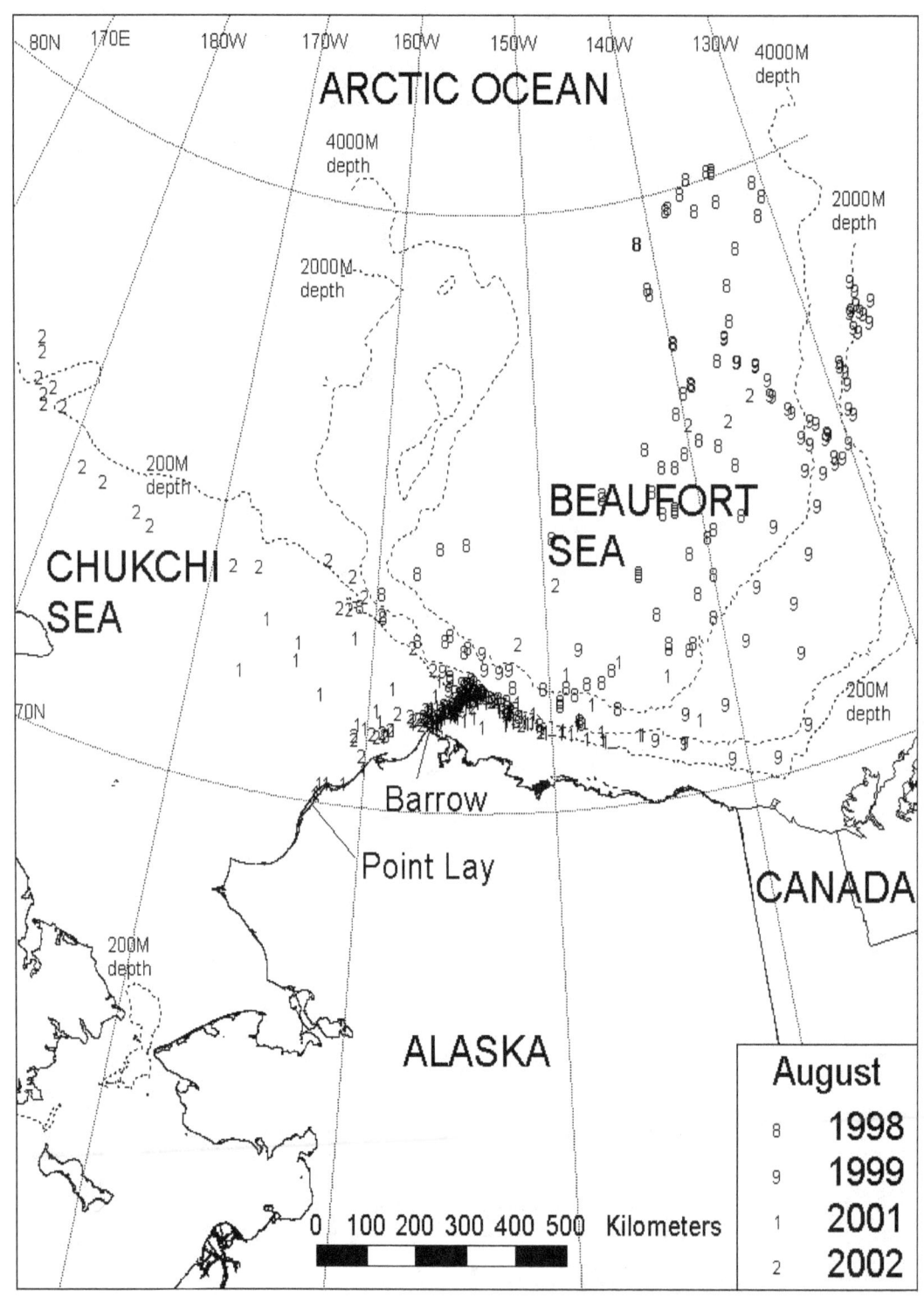

Figure 7. Locations of beluga whales satellite tagged at Point Lay, Alaska, in August 1998–2002. (Each number represents a beluga location; locations for all belugas from each respective year are plotted.)

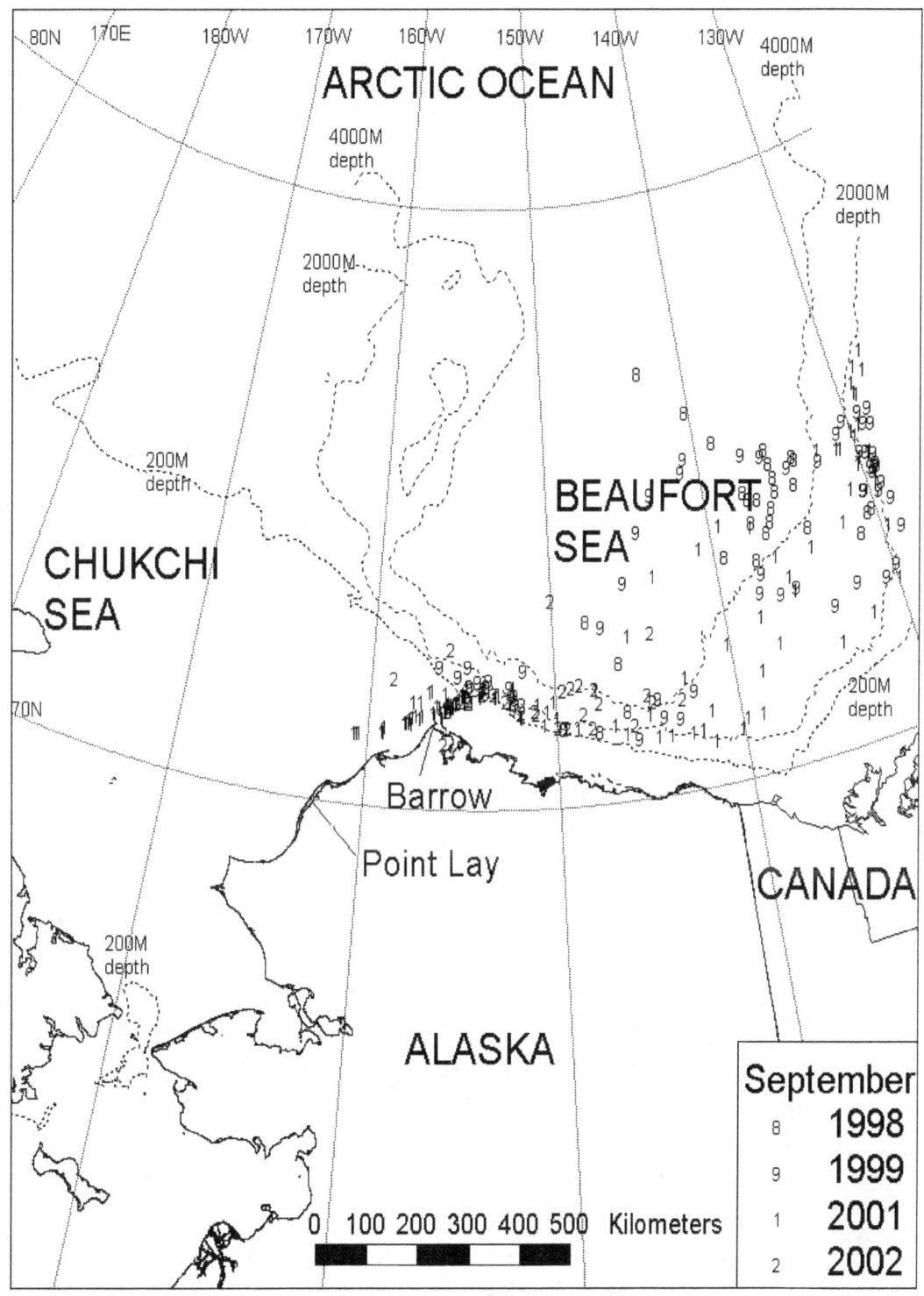

Figure 8. Locations of beluga whales satellite tagged at Point Lay, Alaska, in September 1998–2002. (Each number represents a beluga location; locations for all belugas from each respective year are plotted.)

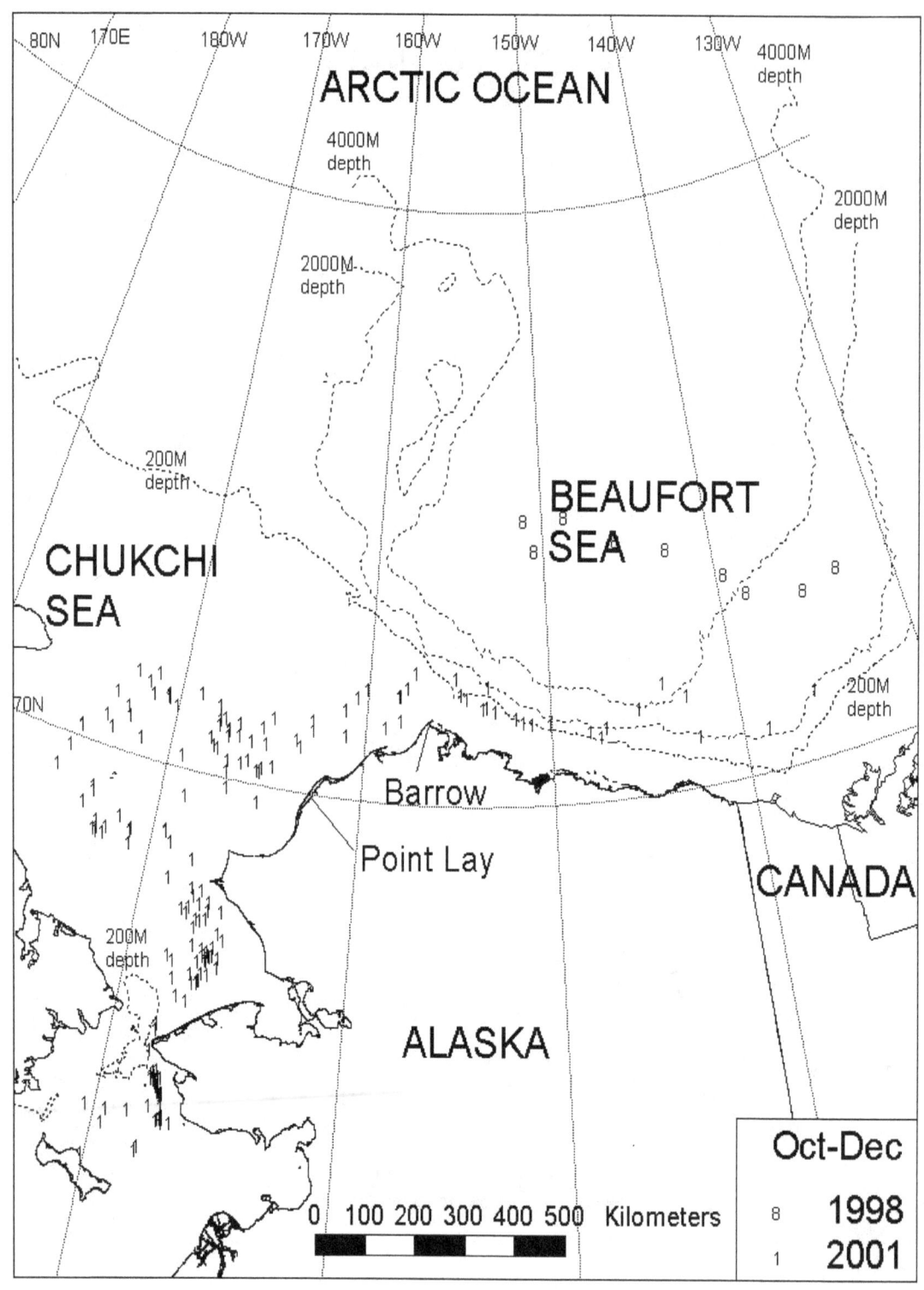

Figure 9. Locations of beluga whales satellite tagged at Point Lay, Alaska, in October–
December 1998–2002. (Each number represents a beluga location; locations for
all belugas from each respective year are plotted.)

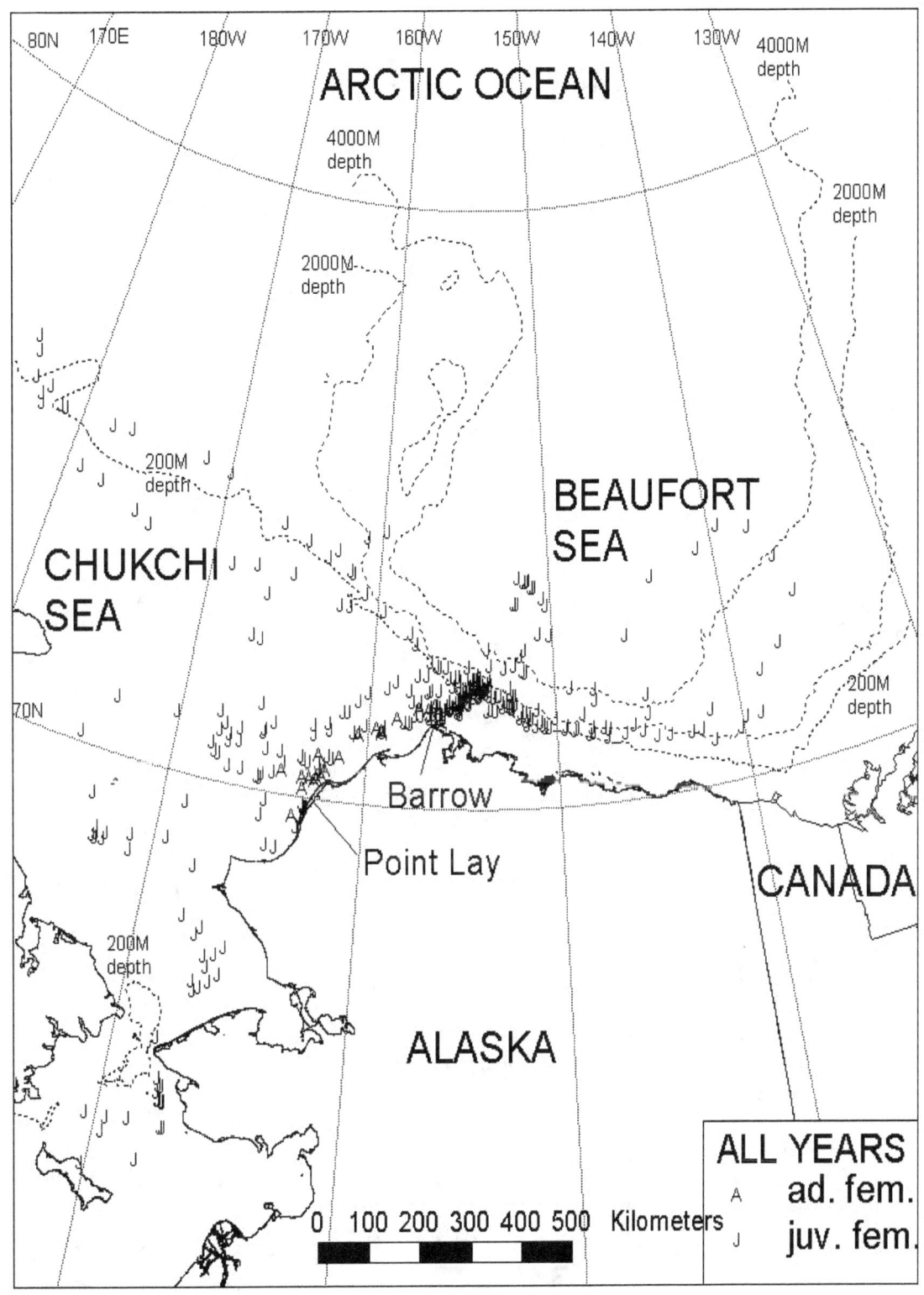

Figure 10. Locations of female beluga whales satellite tagged at Point Lay, Alaska, in 1998–2002, by age class.

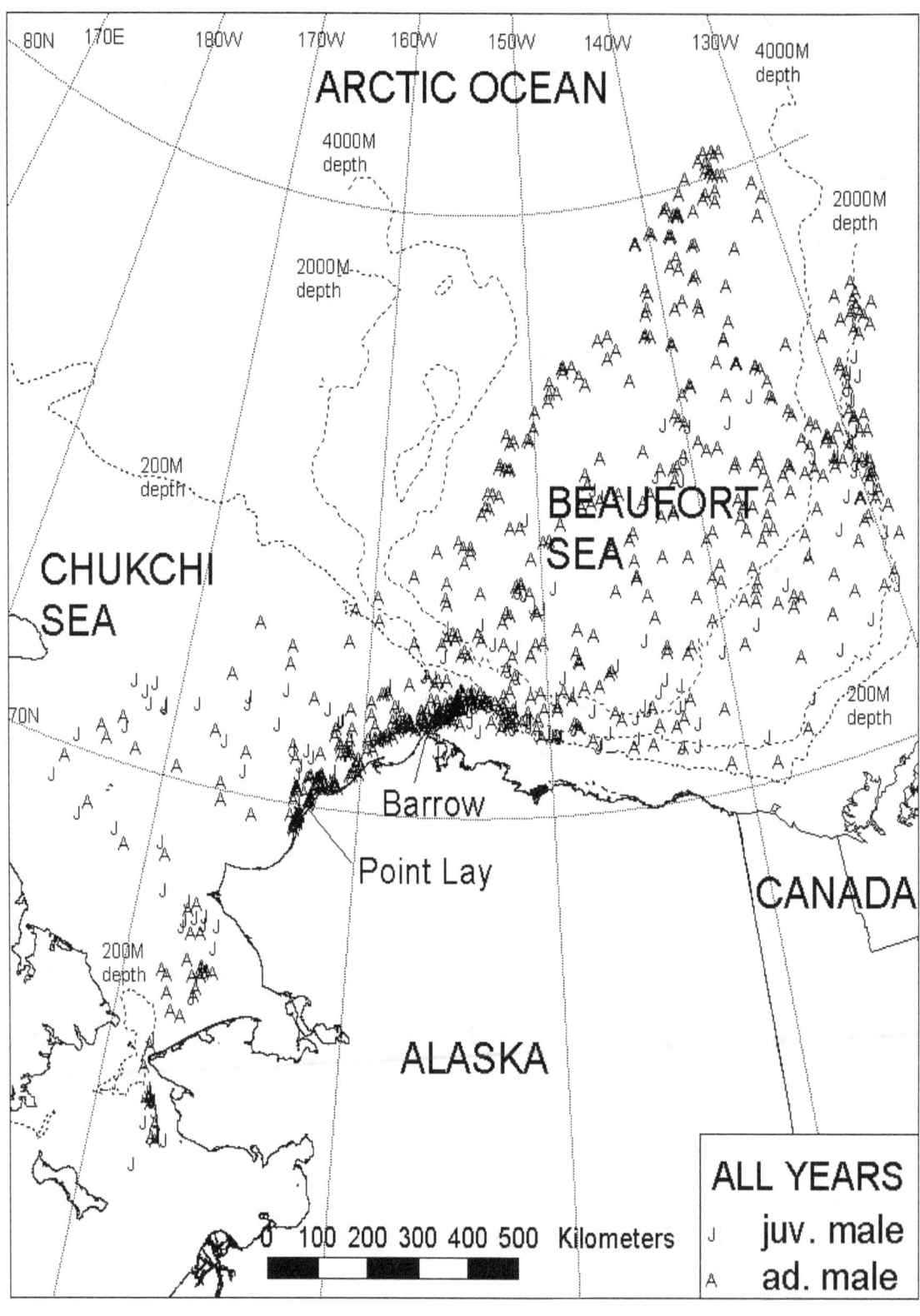

Figure 11. Locations of male beluga whales satellite tagged at Point Lay, Alaska, in 1998–2002, by age class.

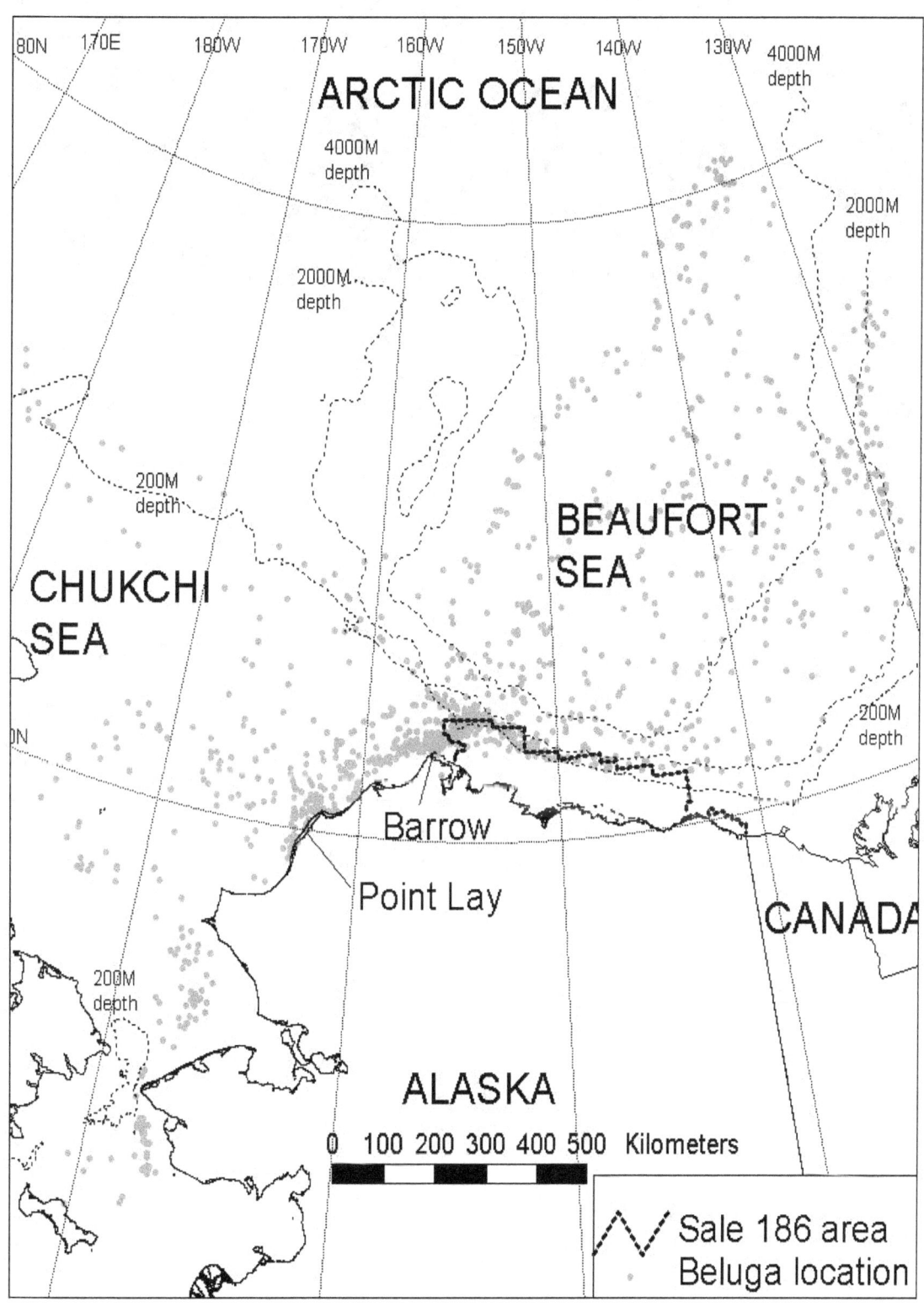

Figure 12. Locations of all beluga whales satellite tagged at Point Lay, Alaska, 1998–2002, in relation of Beaufort Sea OCS lease sale areas (thick dashed line).

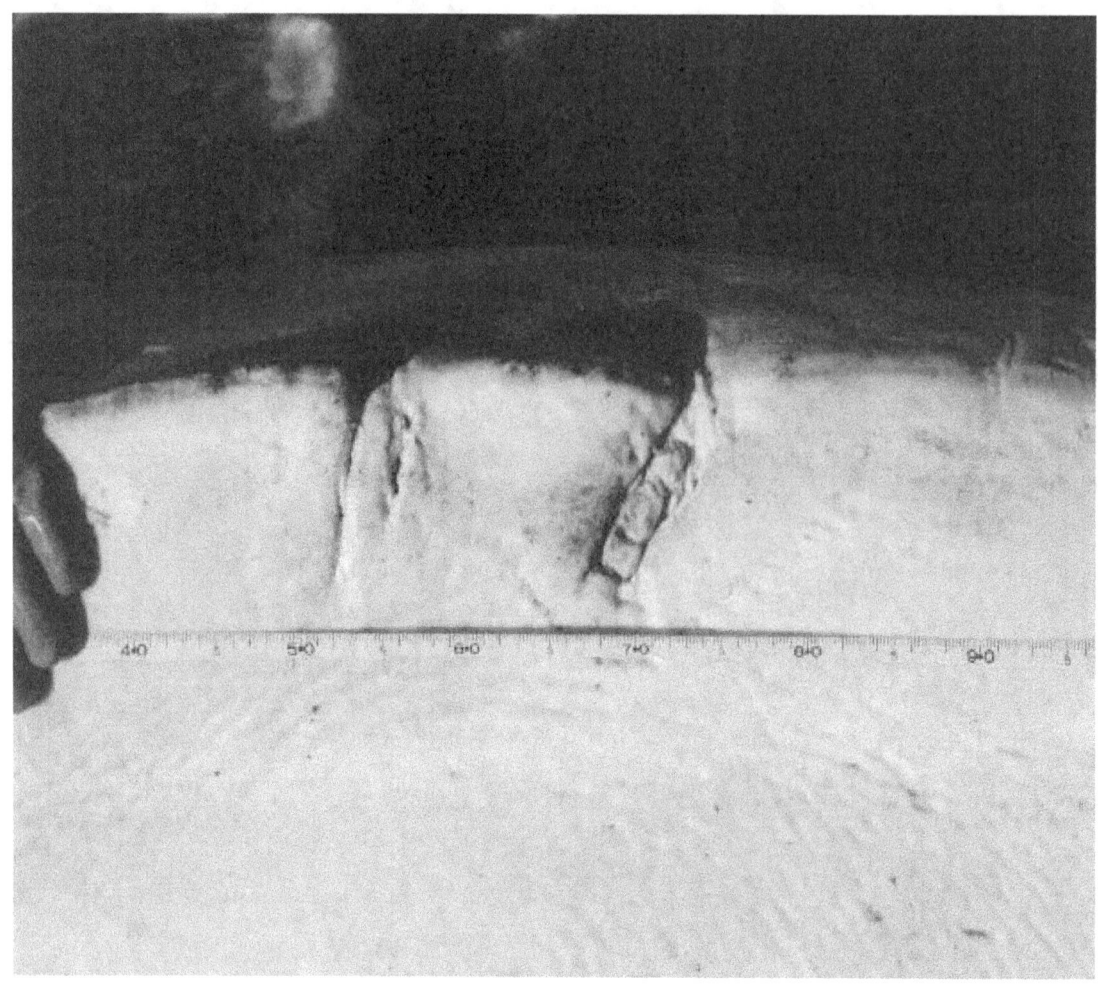

Figure 13. Scars on the dorsum of a beluga at a transmitter attachment site. This animal was taken in a subsistence hunt at Point Lay, Alaska on 30 June 1999 and had been tagged on 29 June 1998.